POSTMODERNITY

JDV Philosophy Series - 4

POSTMODERNITY

An Indian Christian Philosophical Appraisal

Cyril Desbruslais SJ

Edited By
Kuruvilla Pandikattu SJ

Jnana-Deepa Vidyapeeth

&

Christian World Imprints

First Published in 2019 by

Jnana-Deepa Vidyapeeth
Ramwadi, Nagar Road, **Pune-411014**
jdvoffice@jdv.edu.in
www.jdv.edu.in
Phone: +91 20 41036111

&

Christian World Imprints
Christian Publishing & Books from India
H-12 Bali Nagar, **New Delhi-110015**
cwidelhi2017@gmail.com, info@christianworldimprints.com
www.ChristianWorldImprints.com
Phone: +91 11 25465925

ISBN: 978-93-5148-361-8

"Published with the help of the Institute of Missiology – Germany"

Printed in India.

CONTENTS

Editor's Introduction ix
General Introduction xi

PART ONE: MODERNISM 1
Introduction 1
1. What is Modernism? 1
   a. The Renaissance 1
   b. "Modern" Philosophy Surfaces 3
   c. Some Hermeneutics 4
2. Modernist Themes in Detail 5
   a. At Least Two Phases 5
   b. The Anthropological Turn 5
   c. The Primacy of Reason 7
   d. The Dethronement of God and the Spiritual 10
Conclusion 11

PART TWO: SOME KEY POSTMODERNISTS 13
Introduction 13
1. Ferdinand de Saussure (1857-1915) 14
2. Lévy-Strauss (1908-2009) and Structuralism 18
3. Jacques Derrida (1930-2004) 21
4. Jean-Francois Lyotard (1924-1998) 31
5. Michel Foucault (1926-1984) 35
6. Jean Baudrillard (1929-2007) 44
7. Jacques Lacan (1901-1981) 47
8. Some Postmodernist Feminist Thinkers 51

PART THREE: POSTMODERNISM: A SCHOOL OR AN ATTITUDE? 61
1. Anti-Rationalism 63
2. Anti-Subjectivism 64
3. Anti-Humanism 64
4. Some Other Implications 64

PART FOUR: SOME CRITICAL COMMENTS ON POSTMODERNISM 69
1. René Descartes (1596-1650): The Villain of the Piece 69
2. Blaise Pascal (1623-1662): Absolute Rationalism is Irrational 73
3. Jürgen Habermas (1929-): Rehabilitator of Reason 75
4. Ken Wilber (1949-): Rehabilitator of the Subject 77

APPENDICES 89
1. The Action of the Invaders 89
2. Cyril Desbruslais, SJ: A Philosopher of Liberation 93

Glossary 97
Bibliography 105

JDV PHILOSOPHY SERIES - 4

Since 1893 Jnana-Deepa Vidyapeeth has been pioneering philosophy discussion and debate inspired by prominent personalities like Richard De Smet, Jean de Marneffe, Salvino Azzopardi, Cyril Desbruslais, Noel Sheth, John Vattanky, etc. It has been in the forefront of promoting Indian philosophy and making philosophical thinking relevant for contemporary times. In its effort to reach out to like-minded scholars, JDV Philosophy Series has been visualized as a catalyst for interdisciplinary thinking and contemporary exploration on social issues fostering holistic liberation, integral development and creative engagement.

JDV Philosophy Series (Books published so far)

1. Salvino Azzopardi: **Epistemology and Phenomenology of Religions** (2018)
2. Kuruvilla Pandikattu & Thomas Karimundackal (eds): **Melodies from the Flute** (2018)
3. Kurien Kunnumpuram: **Freedom and Joy** (2018)
4. Cyril Desbruslais SJ: **Postmodernity: An Indian Christian Philosophical Appraisal** (2019)
5. Cyril Desbruslais SJ: **Metaphysics Philosophy of Be-ing for Today** (2019)

Books by Cyril Desbruslais SJ

1. Philosophy of Liberation: Revisiting Genuine Religious Experiences with Special Reference to Christianity
2. Postmodernity: An Indian Christian Philosophical Appraisal
3. Metaphysics: Philosophy of Be-ing for Today

EDITOR'S INTRODUCTION

I was privileged to be taught by Prof Cyril Desbruslais in the early 1980's at Jnana-Deepa Vidyapeeth, Pune and he came across to us as a passionate philosopher, whose feet were solidly on the ground. He invited us to think creatively and open our vistas to the needs of the poor and the marginalized, in our philosophical journey. His flair for language, his approachability and dedication was an inspiration for all of us as students.

After my doctorate when I returned to JDV in 1989, during one of our casual chats, I invited him to co-teach a course on postmodernism. Though his main philosophical expertise was on Phenomenology, Existentialism and History of Philosophy, he gladly obliged. He made a personal effort to buy all the books of the postmodern thinkers in French, study them and make them appealing to the students of JDV.

So this book is the product of his commitment and dedication in the early 1990's, when we could feel life fully vibrating in him.

His flair for language, clarity of thought and proficiency both in English and French made the lectures and this book really inspiring and challenging. He was passionately committed to the young and vibe with them. He would go out of his way to reach out to the students and make the philosophical insights easily accessible to them. He cherished being with the young and was a truly inspiring figure.

Personally I am very much indebted to him, since he is the one who has initiated me into the writings of Paul Ricoeur and inspired me to take his hermeneutics and phenomenology for my research, as he has done to countless students.

Unfortunately, he got a mild stroke (Paralytic attack) on October 1, 2016 which has prevented him for functioning as actively and energetically as he used to be. He is able to carry on doing his regular activities, but with some restraint.

While paying homage to my former professor, I want to thank Dr Cyril Desbruslais on behalf of countless students and youth, who have been inspired, challenged and transformed by his life and message.

I also want to thank the communities of De Nobili College, Papal Seminary and Jnana-DeepaVidypeeth where we felt at home, encouraging us to explore, express and empower both critically and creatively. This book is such an adventure by Desbruslais.

Kuruvilla Pandikattu SJ

GENERAL INTRODUCTION

Are you a "Postie"?

"Today, it has become quite fashionable to be a *postie.* To characterize your contribution as 'post-' something else, appears to be a guarantee for relevance, attention and success." So writes Anton A. van Niekirk.[1] And this is natural enough. To prefix your favourite "ism" with a tag like that, would suggest that you're *avant-garde,* a revolutionary trail-blazer, an intrepid breakaway, proposing something startlingly and boldly new. And, by that same token, it would imply that whatever you're coming after (post, remember, is Latin for "after"), has gone out of fashion, is passé, outdated.

Now the latter part of the twentieth century has been particularly prolific in spawning a whole plethora of "posties" – to name a few, there are post-industrialism, post-structuralism and postmodernism. The more observant among us might have noticed that postmodernism is spelt without a hyphen, unlike its two other 'cousins', we might say. Surely, there is a reason for this!

The Missing Hyphen

There is, and it is this. The hyphenated "isms" historically would situate themselves as chronologically "after" the views they qualify. Postmodernism, on the other hand, refers to a tendency, an attitude, a set of values, that vigorously opposed themselves to those upheld by modernism, but postmodernism does not date from after the decline and fall of modernism. It sometimes pre-dated it and even ran concurrently along with it.

Indeed, for this very reason, many scholars are averse to the very term postmodernism (they're not too happy with 'modernism' either, by the way). After all, "ism" words normally conjure up the idea of a school of thought (like rationalism, or empiricism), with a precise set of definite doctrines, upheld, more or less, in common by its major "advocates". But postmodernism (like

1 van Niekirk, Anton A., "Post-Metaphysical versus Postmodern Thinking", in *Philosophy Today* (Summer 1995), p. 171. Quoted by Victor Ferrao, in an unpublished typescript on Postmodernism, p. 1.

modernism) is more a mood or a spirit than a specific doctrine. That is why such authors prefer terms like "modernity" or 'postmodernity'. I am quite aware of this very legitimate concern, but I am sticking to the more generally accepted usage, but I would like to emphasise, right at the outset, I do not wish to suggest that these are "isms" in the regular sense of the word.

What Lies Ahead

That done, let me introduce the four major sections of the book that are now to follow. Part One introduces us to Modernism and what it stands for; after all, without some kind of basic grasp of what modernism is, we would scarce be able to appreciate the postmodernist revolt against it. Then comes Part Two, decidedly the longest and most detailed portion, where we will be introduced to some key postmodernist thinkers and their views. Only then, it is felt, will we be able to best separate out the major themes, concerns and projects of postmodernism. This is what we busy ourselves with in Part Three. This will entail at least a cursory glance at structuralism and post-structuralism, which prepared the ground for postmodernism, as also some other precursors of it. Finally, in Part Four, I will attempt a critical evaluation of this significant movement, with special reference to its relevance for the Third World in general, and for India in particular.

PART ONE

MODERNISM

Introduction

In this brief historical review and reflection, with which I begin my opening chapter, I will first detail my reading of the beginnings of modernism as also how it developed into, or provoked, postmodernism. I am deliberately being rather ambiguous here, though it will be obvious enough what my particular stand on the issue is. This will provide the student with a bird's eye view of how I view modernism and postmodernism, how I see their love-hate relationship as well as prefigure, as it were, my critique of postmodernism. The remainder of this section will be taken up with a more detailed description of what, according to me, are the main themes of modernism.

1. What is Modernism?

A Bit of History

a. The Renaissance

Round about the middle of the fifteenth century there occurred, in Europe, a veritable series of revolutionary events, any one of which would have been enough to convince the most dyed-in-the-wool of cynics or skeptics that a New World Order was being born.

In 1453 Constantinople fell to the Turks (who re-christened it Istanbul) and soon England, France, Germany and the Low Lands were overrun with Christian refugees from that ancient seat of learning. More to the point, they carried along with them precious manuscripts of the classical era that they had managed to salvage from the great library of that city. It was not that the Continent has been totally ignorant of the works of Plato, Aristotle and Homer or of Cicero, Horace and Virgil (and others of their ilk). St Augustine and St

Thomas – and all the Church Fathers – knew and used them in their writings, but it was only to conscript them into buttressing their philosophical theses, as "handmaids of theology." Now, the Greek and Latin Masters were read, studied and appreciated for their own merit.

Then Gutenberg came out with a crude printing press in 1456 and, though it was able to run off a paltry 300 copies a day, that was quite something by those standards and soon identical, accurate copies of key writings were pouring off machines set up in just about every key European city. This came at just the right time, for everyone was eager to have his or her personal copy of the classical texts of the Ancient World and here were they for the asking, replacing the far more expensive, tediously crafted, hard-to-come by and fragile, cumbersome manuscripts. Literacy and learning had become economically viable and these were emancipatory acts in themselves.

As if all that were not enough, in 1492, Columbus discovered a real New World, the earth was circumnavigated and its real size, shape and geography came to be known. Then a long forgotten cosmological theory was revived and it gained credence (at Galileo's cost!). Each of these happening had monumental economic, social, political and religious implications. Taken together, they produced something like an explosion of human thought.

No wonder those people felt they were poised on the threshold of something excitingly new and different. They contemptuously dismissed the preceding two or three centuries as a mere transition period, *media aetas* or Middle Ages or, worse, as The Dark Ages, an obvious reference to the alleged brakes that the all-powerful Roman church had put on creativity and the development of Science and the Arts. They saw themselves as the vanguard of the free, truly modern and they named their times the Renaissance (French for "Re-Birth"), proclaiming a re-birth of knowledge and artistic endeavour, they were convinced that they were striking off towards bold new horizons, making a clean rupture with the past, emancipated from the straitjackets of ecclesiastical and State censors. "Immortal God! What a world I see dawning! Why can I not grow young again!" This remark of Erasmus, in 1517 (he was 53, then) is characteristic and typical of how many felt in those days.[1]

Then reality set in. The Renaissance began with a bang and ended with a whimper. Religious revivals burst upon the scene, "holy wars" broke out on all sides, decimating the populations of several nations-in-the-making. Gunpowder was invented and the Arms Race was on. Great wealth began to be amassed by the powerful few at the cost of the impoverished many: capitalism and colonialism, with all their implications, came into being. If some of the world's greatest works of art and literature date from this time, they were created against a background of nigh universal squalor, social injustice and misery. By 1526 (just ten years before his death and not quite twenty years before the term, *la Renaissance*, had passed into popular usage), Erasmus was a bitter, broken old man, lamenting the demise of his dreams and expectations of a Brave New World.[2] Such was the speedy rise, decline and fall of the first European experiment of modernism.

b. "Modern" Philosophy Surfaces

The second attempt at "modernism", and the one with which postmodernism is associated, came about a century later. It was inaugurated by René Descartes in France (1596-1650) and Francis Bacon in England (1561-1626). Like their Renaissance predecessors, they saw themselves as a new breed and called themselves *moderni*, moderns, to distinguish themselves from the Middle Ages and its ubiquitous Inquisitors. In addition, they had bold and promising developments in the natural sciences to enthuse themselves even further. They also asserted their new found autonomy. They would venture forth boldly, with Science as their guide.

Now much of this was a wholly laudable project and goal and we have much to be grateful for to these intrepid pioneers. But they were far more indebted to, and dependent on, the period they so roundly despised, than they were willing to admit. Descartes and his followers, for one thing, took over a whole gamut of medieval terms and not a few of the arguments that had been deployed by Augustine and company (substance, accident, sufficient reason, various proofs for the existence of God, to mention some) – and with nary a word of acknowledgement – and grafted them onto their "original" insights! And, just for the record, the trend continues, today: Husserl scarce mentions his indebtedness to the Scholastics for his much vaunted "intentionality"! True, Descartes and Bacon would set about replacing Latin with their vernaculars as the medium of discourse, but both of them also wrote in the language of Cicero and Ovid – and quite well, too. One cannot deny that a certain conscious "discontinuity" between the "medievals" and the "modems" was realized by the latter, but it should not be exaggerated.

And let me quickly point out that "modern philosophy" was quite another thing from the heresy (?) condemned by Pope St Pius X in 1907, in his encyclical, *Pascendi*. Though as we will soon note, it was not wholly unrelated to it.

Now, what were those attitudes or concerns that modernism concentrated on, had sought to safeguard amid the light and shade of this fast-moving "modern world"? We will go into this in somewhat detail in a moment, but it will be worth our while to give a broad summary answer to the question, now. And that would be the sense of what we have in common, the fact that there is, beyond the undeniable plurality of our various cultures and traditions, some things which are basic: among these would be a certain shared human make-up, a common psychological infrastructure (conscious and unconscious or id, ego and superego or whatever), the fact that we all find ourselves immersed in the same objective world and that we are able to communicate to each other certain well-defined statements about this reality and, somehow or the other, are able to get across to each other "the message".

However, as we shall see, modernism in its eagerness to affirm and celebrate this commonality, often gave short shrift to the element of diversity. With reckless haste, it tried to convince everyone that this or that trait of its favourite culture (European culture, of course), was that which was "common", "shared" and "basic" to all human beings. As for the non-Europeans, well, if they knew what was good for them, they would obediently admit this to be the case. Invariably, thanks to the dominant position modernist culture found itself in, it foisted a particular brand of uniformity on others and elbowed aside all protests, sacrificing authentic unity in diversity for a convenient canned oneness. And this is where postmodernism comes in.

c. Some Hermeneutics

Postmodernism cautions us against such hasty generalizations. Soon, objections came to be even more strident, not only from the non-European world, but also from minority groups within the European countries: the non-whites, the non-males, the non-Christian peoples. And, in demanding that the voice of the underdog and the marginalized be heeded, it occasionally tended to overshoot the mark and, like Macbeth, 'fall on the other". So concerned with preserving diversity in the face of an all-powerful modernist juggernaut that swallowed up all differences, it often ended up denying that there is anything in common at all, to begin with: no subject, no object, no meaning. An error is an exaggerated truth. Now we should be able to understand the frequent charges of nihilism, skepticism relativism that are frequently levelled against postmodernists!

Taylor and Winquist, in their comprehensive *Encyclopedia of Postmodernism* seem to acknowledge this. They grant that this movement is no mere fad but has "emerged as a significant cultural, political' and intellectual force that defines our era". They also note that critiques levelled against it vary "from eclecticism and montage to neo-skepticism and anti-rationalism" and recognize in it "contradictory, sometimes misguided and various deployments" that invite such criticisms.[3] And David Clippinger, of Pennsylvania State University, in his incisive article, "Modernism", in the same volume, concludes his contribution as follows: "Therefore, modernism might best be conceptualized as a field of ideas, styles and concepts to which the postmodern has returned, carried off and transformed, while simultaneously criticizing what it has chosen to transform and leave behind."[4]

In other words, I do not side with those thinkers who see a radical break between modernism and postmodernism; I see the latter as more of a reconstruction and reinterpretation of the former. Postmodernism seeks to give new meaning to modernism. As Paul Lakeland would put it, "re-writing modernity is what postmodernity is about."[5] The particular angle that I want to give to the debate is the following: At the risk of oversimplification, I would sum up the exchange by saying that modernism tends to exaggerate the element of unity (disregarding diversity), whereas postmodernism overstresses diversity (and denies unity). The more balanced view would be to call for an authentic synthesis of unity in diversity. Admittedly, this is more easily said than done!

2. Modernist Themes in Detail

a. At Least Two Phases

I think we must distinguish at least two phases in modernism, one more rigid and the other providing the transition to postmodernism, its follower cum challenger. The philosophical current, which traces its origins to Descartes and Bacon began a bit more exuberantly as a celebration of rationality, universality and purposive action. Round about the 1900s a certain restlessness begins to set in – especially in the arts. Disharmony, impulsiveness and pastiche work now takes over. Maybe people had gotten a bit bored by the predictability of normative modem art forms. Disharmony, impulsiveness and the irrationality become the guiding spirits. In the still-modernist stage, there is a kind of nostalgic longing for the old days of order and proportion that are ruefully recognized to be on the way out. The advent of postmodernism can be perceived by the fact that this loss is not lamented, but celebrated. The change, subtle at first, appears to manifest itself most strikingly in "modern art", as I have mentioned, and then slowly spreads to other areas – even philosophy and literary criticism. Sometimes it is hard to say where a peculiar art style (e.g. Dadaism) belongs to late modernism or the birth of postmodernism. But there seem to be certain basic outlooks and perspectives that lie at the heart of the modernistic *Weltanschauung* and which postmodernism will challenge, more and more stridently. Let us proceed to detailing them. As a kind of preview, let us recall the five characteristics that Martin Heidegger listed as constituting the modern world view, in his Essay, "The Age of the World Picture."[6] These are the mathematical science of nature, machine technology, the loss of gods, and the attempt at the formation of a universal culture and the conversion of the realm of arts to that of aesthetic experience. He could have included anthropocentrism, which he recognized elsewhere.

b. The Anthropological Turn

Johnson J. Puthenpurackal rightly notes that modernity begins with an explicit turn in thinking: towards human beings.[7] The primacy of the human person is indeed the dynamo that sets in motion the entire machinery of postmodernism.

All other emphases and underscoring derive from this. Heidegger himself admitted this, when he wrote, "The period we call modern ... is defined by the fact that man becomes the centre and measure of all things." And Michel Foucault, perhaps the best known of all postmodernists, made a similar observation when he noted, "the entire philosophical discourse of modernity ... is simply an anthropological intermezzo in the history of thought."[8]

This undeniable anthropological slant in modernism, paradoxically, ended up with a tremendous sense of depersonalization and alienation of the person from the community. This was because it lurched off, uncritically, in the direction of gross individualism. What was worse, the "human" person taken as centre in the modernist perspective was a particular individual (the white, European, male) and all others were measured up against this narrow scale with the result that most were found wanting in the required "humanness" or did their best to become Europeanized Asians, African or Latin Americans, as white and as "Westernly male" as possible. One cannot deny that a good deal of Christian "evangelization" took off from the premise that being unchristian further alienated one from true humanness. The resulting condition is best summarized through the Heideggerian theme of human homelessness. Antony da Silva exposes further aspects of modernism that contribute to, and heightened, this crisis in a particularly poignant way:

> In fact, modernization, with its bias towards a rational, scientific temper, leaves a value vacuum in the lives and identities of many; for example, modernism tends to alienate from traditional life-styles, customs and even belief patterns. Such a psychological dislocation of life invariably leads to self-doubt, insecurity and eventually to an identity crisis.[9]

Much of the latter problems were due, as I have pointed out, to a too narrow and restricted understanding of what constitutes authentic humanness.

Furthermore, the "human person" feted by modernism was, in practice a solitary, isolated ego, such as was discovered and canonized by Descartes and his followers. His *cogito, ergo sum* awarded to the solitary, depersonalized and non-situational ego (invested with the above mentioned white, male, Western and Christian "necessary" qualities) the privileged role of being the sole arbiter of truth and knowledge. Modern philosophy became the philosophy of the nigh-solipsistic subject. No wonder Lévi-Strauss the (post-?)structuralist precursor of postmodernism), in disgust, dubbed the human subject "the spoilt brat of philosophy."[10]

Hard on the heels of this marked individualism, there came a clarion call for freedom, trumpeted by modernism, which saw itself as a prophetic liberator of people from the dead weight of authoritative tradition. Peter Berger draws attention to this when he observes, "the conception of the naked self, beyond institutions and roles, as the end realization of the human being, is the very heart of modernity."[11] The positive side of this is that modernism did, in fact, realize some kind of liberative effect on people (in Europe). Some scholars feel constrained to admit that, were it not for modernism, Western democracy as we know it, would not have emerged in history. M. V. Pylee is one such. He observes: "Although the ideal of democracy was known even centuries before Christ, as a form of political organization, and was tried in isolated small societies, such as the Greek City States, it has never assumed the character of social philosophy, which it has achieved in modern times."[12]

On the negative side, however, it helped usher in consumerism. Together with Cartesian individualism, the seeds of capitalism and consequently a value system based on "having-more", rather than "being-more" fast became the order of the day. As consumerism was augmented by a rising general standard of living, thanks to mass production and *laissez-faire* economies, more and more people suddenly had access to more and more goods and it wasn't long before the meaning and purpose of human existence was seen to consist of an ever widening and rapidly increasing range of material goods. The media played a key role in convincing people that they needed certain commodities and the mechanisms of fashion and built-in obsolescence were recruited to create demand, together with the "keeping-up-with-the Joneses" (or Desais or Mukerjees?) syndrome. Children were made to feel that their parents didn't really care for them if they weren't gifted with the latest pair of Adidas sneakers or iPhones. Globalization cashed in on modernism.

c. The Primacy of Reason

The focus on the human subject in the narrow sense of the term, thanks to Descartes, led to the deification of reason, that faculty which was supposed to be the attribute of the human species par excellence. This kowtowing to abstract reason, segregated from human embodiedness, from the community and the world around us, led to the rise of a certain naïve objectivism (the power of human reason is that it enables us to know things just as they are) and hence the quest for certainty and absolute knowledge (which, as a sort of corollary, had to be universal, too) was launched.

Thus, Descartes, the founding-father of Modern Philosophy lamented that though philosophy had been "cultivated for many years by the most distinguished men", "yet there is not a single matter within its sphere which is not still in dispute."[13] Hence he resolved to find a starting- point so sure and indubitable that not even the most radical of skepticisms would be able to shake it. 'If only philosophy could be as curtain as that great paradigm of all knowledge that is one, true, certain and universal: mathematics!' That was the unspoken refrain that directed him and his disciples. He was quite convinced that the 'cogito' provided him with that. One of his earliest followers, Spinoza, wrote a text book on *Ethics*, presenting the matter in the form of *axiomata*, proofs, corollaries and diagrams – in short *modo geometrico,* as he would call it – as this would capture those desirable qualities of Mathematics and Geometry and assure for his work eternal and universal readership. Shades of Plato and the yearning for all that is "eternal and everlasting"!

Having sought and found (as he was quite convinced) a secure foundation for all human knowledge with his "first philosophy" and its basis, which had yielded him an infallible criterion of eternal, and unchanging truth ("a clear and distinct idea"), Descartes felt himself responsible for providing every discipline with an equally unassailable foundation. Thus foundationalism was born (the resolve to ensure that every branch of knowledge be established on an incontestably certain foundation) and philosophy was identified with epistemological concerns.

Inseparable from all this was the birth of scientism, the conviction that all disciplines, including philosophy and the arts, should attain respectability in the only way open to them: by proving that they were exact sciences, dispelling all doubt and uncertainty. The father of contemporary thought, Immanuel Kant (1724 – 1804) was in full agreement. He even went one step further: the paradigm would not be the abstract Cartesian "science" of Mathematics, but the more down to earth positive science of astronomy. And when he coined his rallying cry, *Sapere Aude!* [Dare to Know!] he was not only asserting the autonomy of human reason from all control of State and Church but was assuring us that, with a little (or morel) effort and perseverance, there is no mystery in the universe that we'd not be able to solve and decipher in clear cut, scientific exactitude. Rational and scientific came to be synonyms in the popular mind. Thus scientific exactness, mathematical rigour, pure objectivity and relentless universality – all of which were seen to be undeniable properties of the positive sciences – were required to be the hallmark of any knowledge worthy of the name.

Soon everything (with some sections of the populace not far behind) was seen as but a means to make more gain. Scientism had led to many technological breakthroughs which were an undeniable boon for the many, but it also gave us capitalism, an economic ideology that preaches human liberation and happiness through increased productivity and production: having more, culminating in increased GNP and profit. Rapid urbanization, the mushrooming of what Charles Dickens would call "dark, Satanic mills", the ugly, pollution-spewing factories that dehumanized and animalized so many workers in the nineteenth century, as Marx has described – all this is the direct legacy of early modernism. Panikkar's phrase "growing technocracy" is a good summing up of the human social displacement, unhygienic conglomerations of "workers' flats" and the disruption of human relatedness with our fellows and with nature, that was the cruelty of technology then – and which still remains so in many parts of the globe.

Again, modernism – for all its high-sounding rant about universalization and equality – brought about all manner of divisions, fragmentations and disparity. Modernism went hand-in-hand with industrialization, which was built on mass production and that entailed division of labour and specialization. People were locked into isolated and specific roles. Then along came what Richard J. Bernstein called "the iron cages of bureaucratic rationality", from whose clutches we have yet to break free.[14] Modernity is not unrelated to the development of the military as a specialized aspect of the nation-state. The introduction of the uniform, drills and parades, as well as the division into strict hierarchies of rank were all carried out to ensure more efficient discipline and co-operation, so as to enforce speedier obedience from all. Such military patterns of organization and smooth running seem to have percolated into the civilian world as well – into industry, commerce and political administration. It would seem that it also inspired the Church in its attempts to ensure worldwide regimentalization, with the Curia arranged in proper military lines of protocol and order. These divisions and differentiations began to penetrate society to such an extent that it was not unusual for an individual to find himself hard put to play his or her multifarious roles as professional, spouse, friend, believer, and so on, without strict compartmentalization so as to avoid clashes between his or her various personae. We are told that Michael Faraday said that when he opened the door of his laboratory, he closed the door of his oratory. People started to wear masks to suit their various roles and lost touch with a sense of inner personal responsibility.

Finally, whatever modernism had inherited from the Enlightenment, together with all the baggage it accumulated over the years – be it values, beliefs, principles, moral directives, etc. – was taken to be universal, not just in the abstract sense, but also as something universalisable: something that just had to be accepted and integrated into the thinking and practice of all human beings everywhere.[15] Thus, European culture ("Enlightenment Culture!) was understood as more "civilized" and fit for general assimilation than, say, Indian or Japanese culture, which, it was felt, would do well to slough off their own and take them on. Kipling spoke of the "White Man's Burden", the responsibility of the nobler Caucasian races to correct and elevate the barbarous customs and traditions of the non-white savages. Panikkar referred to this type of colonial thinking as an attempt at a gross "monoformism" of culture (i.e. the resolve to give one single Western/"Christian" shape to the rich plurality of world cultures).

Max Weber (1864-1918) qualified modernism as the first rationalization of society. Having exiled all "spirits and demons" from the daily life of the simple people (which was a very good thing, to be sure), it also exorcised the sense of mystery and wonder from Nature. A cold, calculating and manipulative attitude now began to govern the individual's relations with the other, be it his or her fellow humans or the environment. Primacy of place was awarded to efficiency and productive organization in more and more aspects of life. Whether it be increased crop yields, more military precision, the automation of the household or coordinating airline schedules, rationalization began to penetrate the depths of the social fabric as the only relevant way to promote relationships.

d. The Dethronement of God and the Spiritual

This was the inevitable corollary of the enthronement of human reason. Investing human reason with omnipotence and infallibility was tantamount to its deification. Freud had already hailed, "Our God, Logos, or Reason and so there was no room for any other Absolute. Paulos Mar Gregorious, also recorded this development, when he detected as "the fundamental act of the Modern, the repudiation of the transcendent and its replacement by human rationality as sovereign, and as the new unifying principle of all experience and all understanding."[16]

The American theologian, John Cogley, adverted to this phenomenon when he wrote, "Religion is scriptural and credal. Modernity, on the other hand, tends to be pragmatic, naturalistic and spontaneous."[17]

Secularity (not to be confused with secularism, which recognizes the legitimate autonomy of the State from religious control) now began to make its inroads felt. It propagated a view of religion as a mass of quaint, outdated superstitions, founded on oppressive and dogmatic assertions and unworthy of a truly "modern" person. The modernist saw it has his or her special responsibility to liberate deluded people from the clutches of religion. There was no God and no hereafter. All that mattered was the "here and now". This is the "Gospel of Consumerism", of human fulfillment consisting in the enjoyment of material goods and pleasures during our lifespan on this planet (which we must seek to prolong as much as possible). One of the dogmas of this New Creed (for such it was, peddling itself as a "self-evident truth" that neither needed – nor could – be justified) was the belief in the inevitability of Progress without End. The religious world view in general, and the Christian in particular, involved an acceptance of divine providence and a certain purposiveness in history. Modernism rejected the idea of God, but retained the conviction of the purposiveness of history, which it saw as a naturally forward movement, naturally and spontaneously surging upwards, with everyone and everything inevitably getting better and better with the march of time. It is perhaps this ability of modernism to provide a hope and vision for future generations that kept it alive, despite many setbacks it experienced due to its naïve assumptions.

Conclusion

Modernism, thus, offers us a mixed bag of attainments. No sincere person can deny that it helped provide a happier, more comfortable lifestyle for very many people in a very short time – and that is no mean achievement. This blinded most of us to the crippling and negative elements that had become part of the packaged deal. But it was all too easy to be mesmerized by the promise of an "ever better life" held out to us. No wonder that the automobile, the train, the airliner and supersonic travel (not to mention the latest in Information Technology) should become symbols of progress and modernity. If I have sounded overly negative in my comments, it is only because I want to shock us into an awareness of the need to discriminate. We should not let ourselves be so "sold" by the benefits of modernism so as not to notice, or pay scant attention to, its alarming side. There is yet one more reason for my having come down so hard on modernism. That is because Descartes and Company did such a shabby job of high-lighting what is in common: they offered their post modernistic critics such a caricature of subjectivism, objectivity and grand narratives that it was all too easy to demolish these inanities ... and then assume that there was no alternative, more authentic, understanding of these same ideas left!

Endnotes

1 For more details about the excitement, followed by disillusionment, that the Renaissance unleashed among all and sundry, see my notes on *Modem Philosophy*. Mimeographed Text (no date), Pune, Jnana-Deepa Vidyapeeth, p. 99.

2 Huxley, Aldous. *Brave New World,* New York: Spark Publishing, 2014.

3 Taylor, Victor E. and Charles E. Winquist (editors), *Encyclopedia of Postmodernism.* London, Routledge, 2001, "Introduction", p. xiii.

4 Ibid. p. 252.

5 Lakeland, Paul, *Postmodemity: A Christian Identity in a Fragmented World.* Minneapolis, Fortress Press, 1997, p. xii (quoted by Ferrao, OP. Cit.. p. ii).

6 Quoted by David Kolb, *The Critique of Pure Modernity: Hegel, Heidegger and After.* Chicago, The University of Chicago Press, 1986, p. 121.

7 Puthenpurackal, Johnson J. "Postmodernity and its Effects of Metaphysics", a paper presented to the Association of Christian Philosophers of India (October 27-29 October, 1999), p. 1.

8 Quoted by Puthenpurackal, p. 1.

9 da Silva, Antony, "Combatting Communalism in Twenty-First Century India: A Social Psychological Perspective", *Jnanadeepa: Pune Journal of Religious Studies*. Vol. 2, No. 1 (January 1999), p. 80.

10 Quoted by Madan Sarup, *An Introductory Guide to Post-Structuralism and Postmodernism.* Athens, Georgia, The University aof Georgia Press, 1993, p. 1.

11 Quoted Kolb, Op. Cit.. p.

12 Pylee, M. V., "Religion and the Modernist Movement," in Thomas Paul (ed) *Present Day Challenges to Religion*, Alwaye, Pontifical Institute of Theology and Philosophy, 1973, p. 32.

13 Descartes, Rene, *Discourse on Method. Part I* (my translation), quoted Desbruslais, Op, Cit.. p. 117.

14 Kolb, op. cit. p. 7.

15 Kolb, Op. Cit.. p. 7. See also Gregorios, Paulos Mar, "Modern, Postmodern, and the Future of the Humanity: Nostalgia for the Unattainable." http://www.paulosmargregorios.in/Work_of_Mar_Gregorios/English%20Articles/Humanity/ modern_postmodern.htm

16 Gregorios, Paulos Mar, "Modern, Postmodern, and the Future of the Humanity: Nostalgia for the Unattainable." http://www.paulosmargregorios.in/Work_of_Mar_Gregorios/English%20Articles/Humanity/ modern_postmodern.htm

17 Quoted by M. V. Pylee, Op. Cit.. p. 38.

PART TWO

SOME KEY POSTMODERNISTS

Introduction

Apparently, the first recorded use of the term "postmodern" was by a certain Rudolf Pannwitz (in German), in 1917, in his study on the *Crisis of European Culture*.[1] He used it, there, to refer to an "athletically hardened, nationalistically conscious, military trained, religiously exalted" type of person who has recently "emerged from the great decadence of the radical revolution of European nihilism."[2] A chilling anticipatory glimpse of the Nazi hordes, if ever there was one! The same word was utilized in 1934, this time in a totally different context: to designate a school of Hispanic literature, dating from the period 1905-1914.[3] Perhaps its first usage in English was in the comments Dudley Pitts appended to his *Anthology of Latin-American Poetry*.[4] It also appears in Arnold Toynbee's *A Study of History*, where he applied it to western industrial society after 1875.[5] It attained a certain notoriety in the 1960s as the qualification of certain avant-garde artists and critics of a somewhat Bohemian lifestyle. It had made forays into religion much earlier, notably is the writings of Bernard Iddings Bell (1886-1958), an American Christian author, Episcopal priest, and conservative cultural commentator, who, in the late 1930s wrote several books of an-apologetic nature, directed at postmodernists in particular.[6]

The kind of "postmodernists" that will command our attention in this study will be, not so much those of a literary or artistic bent, but rather those thinkers that sought to "justify plurality and multiplicity in art and aesthetics."[7] Such writers were motivated with the very self-conscious resolve to respond to the legacy of the Enlightenment which, to them, appeared to be putting a spoke in the wheels of progress by clinging tenaciously to certain outdated ideals.

Though scholars nowadays seem to leave no stone unturned in their eagerness to recruit postmodernists from just about every nation and age

(Nietzsche and Heidegger are most commonly cited, but Shakespeare, St. Augustine and Jesus are not far behind), I will begin with a rather unpretentious man, who hardly saw himself as a radical or a revolutionary and then move on to the others whom he inspired and provoked (whether he intended it or not) to throw themselves into this line of bold and innovative thinking.

1. Ferdinand de Saussure (1857-1915)

Saussure and Linguistics

Ferdinand de Saussure was a Swiss academician, distinguished in a – at time – rather exotic and obscure discipline, linguistics. Born in Geneva on November 26, 1857, he went on to study Chemistry, Physics, a bit of Theology and, much later, languages, securing his doctorate from Leipzig in 1880. In 1891 he was appointed Professor of Sanskrit and Indo-European Languages at the University of Geneva and passed an uneventful life in that orderly city, plodding from his lodgings to his lectures and research and back, publishing only one work in his life-time, a rather specialized monograph on the vowel system of the Indo-European languages. He died in the city he was born, on February 22, 1913, and earned a niche for himself in history some years after he was buried.

From 1907 to 1911 he had taught a course on linguistics which, after his death, his students put together in a now famous and epoch-making book, *Course on General Linguistics*.[8] It was this book that helped to rescue linguistics from being a pottering historico-descriptive record of how various languages develop, influence each other and change over their time of existence and made of it a full-fledged and respectable scientific discipline, in its own right. He did this by focusing on a study of the patterns and functions of language in contemporary usage, with the stress on how meaning is established and also on how linguistic structures work. What he said about language may not, at first, seem to be very earth-shattering, but the conclusions some of his followers and detractors drew from them (legitimately or not) were, by any standards, quite revolutionary!

We could conveniently summarize the main points he made about words into three brief statements, or *sutras* (to use a typically Indian turn of phrase). Let us proceed to state them and add a brief explanatory note to each.

a. Words are ARBITRARY

That is to say, there is no rational or logical explanation as to why a particular word should be used to refer to a thing. Words are "unmotivated signs", as Saussure says, and there is no inner link which binds them to their respective objects. It is sheer arbitrary choice that makes us use "horse", where a German would say, "Pferd" a Frenchman "cheval" and a Hindi-speaker "ghoda". Of course, there are a few words in every language that are given to objects because they imitate a sound that is made, for example hiss and miao in English. But these "onomatopoeic" words are relatively scarce and they vary in different languages.

(So here, too, one could contest the "objectivity" of what people have been hearing; the "sound", it would appear was more in the ear of the hearer than in the alleged object making the noise); once again the "link with reality" seems to be severed. For example, an English speaker is quite convinced that he hears a dog say "bark" or "bow-wow", whereas a Frenchman would argue in favor of "aboie" or "ouaf".

b. Words are RELATIONAL

That is to say words relate, or refer to, not things but to other words. Language is a self-contained entity, which is quite independent of, and unrelated to, "reality", the world of objects and things around us.

This means that a word cannot be defined in isolation from other words (which means, implicitly, that it can be defined in isolation from things. Sometimes words derives its meaning from its place on a *syntagmatic chain* (Saussure's phrase), that is, a list of words that have some connection, or relation, with each other. For example, let us take the syntagmatic list, hovel – shack – hut – house – mansion – palace. We might have noticed that this catalogue is arranged in ascending order, with the most miserable dwelling place (hovel) beginning the chain, which culminated in the most magnificent one (palace) in the end, the others being each a step higher than the preceding. Indeed, each of the words depends for its precise meaning on the exact position it occupies in the chain; for example, a "hut" is better than a "shack", but not quite good as a "house". Its position *differentiates* it (another key Saussurean term) from the others. Then, again, other words are defined in terms of their "paired opposites". Saussure calls them *dyads*; others prefer to say *binaries*. Examples would include any word, mention of which seems, nigh automatically to summon up its contrary in our minds man/woman, night/day, good/bad and so on. One of the pairs is usually (and most conveniently) defined in terms of its opposite; "man" means "not-woman", "night" means "not-day" and so on. Whence Saussure comes out with a sentence that would be well exploited by many of his followers (post-, structuralists and postmodernists), not always wisely, "In a language there are only differences, without fixed terms."[9] In a now (in)famous example, in his *Course*,[10] Saussure gave an illustration as to how there are no fixed meanings in language: the 8.25 express train from Geneva to Paris. Every day that train leaves for Paris, but what gives it its identity? It's a different engine with a different set of carriages, different passengers and different service crew. It may even leave late and still it's called "the 8.25 express from Geneva."

Saussure's conclusion is that it's only its position in a structure of differences that gives the train its identity: it's after the 7.25 train and before the 9.25 one: its identity is purely relational. In the same way he asks how a street, say, "Straight Street" has its identity. One may change the buildings in it over the years, rebuild the entire street, widen it so that more traffic may ply, the people who live on it may change, and the shops, etc., may also become different. And yet we call it Straight Street: not because anything in it gives it an identity but because of its position, say, at right angle between "X Street" and MY Road". Once again its identity is purely relation – all Many structuralists, post-structuralists and postmodernists would draw all kinds of extreme conclusions from these observations, without pausing for a moment to ask whether they would stand up to critical judgment.

c. Words are CONSTITUTIVE of meaning of the world: In other words, meaning is something we give to objects; it is not something contained in the thing: our mind gives meanings to things. Well-known examples of this would be "terrorist" and "freedom" fighter: which of these two terms you use to refer to someone depends not so much on what he does, but how you view what he does! Think also of what an RSS man and a fundamentalist Christian mean when they use the word, "conversion": they see reality differently and so they respond to it differently.

It used to be said that there are three versions of every story: your version, my version and the truth. Nowadays (after Saussure) we may be a bit hesitant as to what to call "the truth". After all, all the available terms we use are linguistic and all are thereby constitutive of meaning: there is no neutral position, for there is not truth about anything which stands outside of language (which is what it would have to do to be really neutral).

It begins to appear that all language constitutes or constructs the world, not merely reflect it, as we naïvely might have though once. We divide up the points of the compass into four basic directions: North, South, East and West. But the panorama that surrounds us does not break itself up into four points. It runs continuously around us in an unbroken circle. We make it divide up into four segments; we could just as easily have divided it up into five or six points!

Thus Saussure's *Course* taught that language functions in a way which is arbitrary, relational and constitutive. This way of thinking about language was seized upon by the structuralists, for it offered them a model of a system (structure) which is self-contained, one in which individual items relate to other items within the set-up and thus create larger structures, without having to reach beyond themselves to "the world", "reality" or "objects"! Now, there are a few more relevant Saussurean notions to clarify.

i) *Langue* vs *parole*; The former refers to language as a system or a structure (grammar with its various rules that have to be observed so as to make a coherent statement) and the latter designates an utterance, that is, what I want to say. For instance, if I want to say, "The cat is on the mat", that is my parole (what I want to say). Now I must decide whether I should say this in English, Hindi or Marathi (this would depend primarily on the person I want to speak to; if he/she only under-stand English, there is no point in trying to say it in Marathi. Well, if I say that in English, I must follow a different set of grammatical rules than if I were to say it in Marathi or Hindi; these different sets of grammatical rules are what is meant by langue. If a person is ignorant of thc langue of Marathi, he/she would be unable to either speak or understand something said in that language.

ii) *Signifier* vs *signified*: At first sight, we, quite naturally might think that these means "word" and "object", respectively. But remember, these are Saussurean terms and language for him is a closed system, complete in itself and not having to go out of itself to point to reality, with which it has no internal link, anyway (words are arbitrary, don't forget!) That would be wrong. For Saussure, signifier is not so much a word as a "sound-image". Sounds are momentary and link up with other sounds: memory links up sound-images so as to make sense. As for "signifier", this is the "mental-image" (what we would perhaps call the "idea" or "concept". Thus, language remains a closed system. So signified is the "mind image" (the concept), in contrast to the signified, the "sound image" (the spoken word).

iii) *Syntagmatic* vs *paradigmatic axes*: Incidentally, the noun form of syntagmatic is syntax and that of paradigmatic is paradigm and the "axes" mentioned are the plural of axis (a kind of imaginary line, about which a thing is thought to rotate), not axe! Syntax refers to the way words are arranged in a sentence: by changing their order, we influence the meaning of the parole horizontally. If, instead of saying, "The cat is on the mat", I exchange the positions of the second and last words and say, "The mat is on the cat", I have changed the meaning of the sentence – horizontally. I make a paradigmatic change when I replace one word with another (which is not quite its synonym), a word which has different associations, e.g. I replace "dinghy" with "yacht" or "hovel" with "mansion". When I do this, I change the meaning of a parole vertically. This opens the door to all kinds of creativity with words: puns, allusions and so on.

Comment: Saussure has certainly given us food for thought and taught us to be less naïve about our preconceived glib convictions about objectivity and neutrality. But, does he not sometimes overstate his point? An error, after all, is an exaggerated truth and there are at least two such that I must allude to, at least in passing, before we go a step further.

In the first place, does it make sense to posit a category of pure difference? As the critic, Christopher Ricks, so pointingly asked, can you have pure difference, without difference between things?[11] And then there is the 8.25 express train. Is its identity given to it solely by its position on the time-table? As Peter Barry puts it in *Beginning Theory*:

> A counter-argument might be that the 8.25 has to be a train before it can be the 8.25: nobody will remark, 'There goes the 8.25 to Paris' if a flock of pigeons emerges from under the station canopy: likewise, it is true to say that a given street has a largely relational identity – you define 'X' Street by saying that it's the one that runs at right angles between 'Y' Street and 'Z' Street. All the same, a piece of string stretched between the two will not be mistaken for the street.[12]

It is good to note down these reservations at the outset. Other thinkers, for whatever reason, have not been so perceptive or critical and have carried postmodernism to its logical conclusions into all manner of nihilism, skepticism and relativism, it is worth underlining where things began to go wrong in the first place.

2. Lévy-Strauss (1908-2009) and Structuralism

Claude Lévy-Strauss was born at Brussels (Belgium) in 1908. He occupied the Chair of Social Anthropology at the Collège de France and was elected member of the Acadamie Française.

He was responsible for taking a theory in linguistics and showing it could explain how all systems work. Thus, structuralism was born, which might be pinned down to the conviction that things cannot be understood in isolation – they have to be seen in the context of the larger structures they are part of. Lévy-Strauss applied Saussure's linguistic insights to the study and interpretation of myths, thus earning for himself the title of "Father of Structuralism". He suggested that the individual tale (parole!) from a cycle of myths did not have a separate inherent meaning of its own; rather, it could only be understood by considering its position within the whole cycle of related myths (langue!), especially in terms of the similarities and differences it revealed with others in the sequence. Lévy-Strauss was delighted: he was quite convinced that he had chanced upon a scientific method, comparable to that of the physical sciences, which he could make good use of and thereby ensure the respectable scientific status of sociology. He went on to write his *Anthropological Study of Myths*, in 1955, following it up, in I960, with *Le Geste d'Asdiwal*[13] which laid the secure foundations for the scientific study of mythology.

Others followed his methodology, with noteworthy results. Vladimir Pop brought out a structuralist study of *The Morphology of the Folk Tale* and Roland Barthes applied Levy-Strauss' method to a study of general modern culture. In *Mythologies* he submitted to intellectual analysis things like the difference between boxing and wrestling, eating steak and chips, the cinema image of a popular actress' face and so on. Each of these was situated against a wider structure of values, beliefs and symbols, as the key to understanding their deeper import. For instance, he noted that boxers, by convention, do not cry out with pain in "the ring" when hit, but wrestlers do, the latter often disregard the rules, while the former do not and – as anyone who has watched WWF will corroborate – unlike the boxer, who fights as himself, the wrestler does so in the elaborate guise and hype of a make-believe villain and hero. While wrestlers rant and snarl aggressively, stage elaborate displays of agony and triumph, threaten each other with all kinds of melodramatic speeches, boxers fight doggedly and perseveringly without any playing to the gallery. Clearly, concludes Barthes, these two sports have two different roles within society: boxing celebrates the brave endurance with which we must face the trials of life, whereas wrestling symbolizes the eternal and ultimate struggle between good and evil in which we are all involved.[14] This is classical structuralism: the individual item is "structuralised" or "con-textualised by structure" and, in doing so, layers of significance are revealed. The "wider structures" into which "the text" must be inserted so as to discern its deeper meaning, could be anything from the entire corpus of an author's writings, to the cultural traditions and values to which it belongs, or even the particular genre which it re-enacts or parodies. What is crystal clear is that, for Levy-Strauss, the text is a cultural artefact. He further emphasized that there was a subtle and unconscious socialization of the human person at work through linguistic structures. Nietzsche's slogan, "God is dead" is "now old hat" he exclaimed. Now we must proclaim, "Man is dead!" For the human person is but a construct. It is structures like language that produce humans, not the other way round.

Then came 1968 and the French student uprising. Striking workers were joined by thousands of students, chanting, *"A bas le structuralism!"* [Down with Structuralism!]. Structuralists were beginning to be seen as fuddy-duddies who, for all their revolutionary cant, were quite committed to upholding and supporting the old structures, when new ones were called for. Structuralism was out and post-structuralism was in and Lévy-Strauss, most obediently, complied. He refused to have anything to do with structuralism and distanced himself from it very explicitly, especially in his later writings, such as *The View, from Afar*.[15] Structuralism had escaped Lévy-Strauss' control and eventually developed into post-structuralism, but there was no denying that both of these trends would become forces to reckon with in the Western understanding of knowledge.

Move towards Post-Structuralism

Post-structuralism is not so much a "further development" of structuralism as a radical revolt against it. This does not mean that the post-structuralists assert that structuralism and its premises are wrong. On the contrary, their contention is that the structuralists lack either the intelligence to see trifler revolutionary implications or lack the courage to draw the logical conclusions that their basic ideas warrant.

Now, one of the central convictions of structuralism is that Language Constructs the World, it doesn't merely reflect it: how we see is what we see. If this is so, the post-structuralists argue, then we are cast adrift in an uncertain world. We have no secure and stable centres of reference to "give us a local habitation and a name", as Shakespeare would put it. Ours is a radically de-centred universe, for the fact that language makes (constitutes) our world, means that all our formerly smug and solid "centres" turn out to be mere "constructs", unconscious mental fabrications and not objective terms of reference. In other words, they have been "deconstructed" (a key post-structuralist terra): they have been shown up for the artificial, "constructed" things they are: we can peel away their man-made skins as we might do to onions.

If we persist in removing layer after layer from an onion, eventually we are left with nothing. What had previously seemed to us so solid and real dissolves into emptiness. This is what happens when we deconstruct our constructs. Either they turn out to be smaller and not so powerful and impressive after all, or they ultimately vanish before us into nothingness. Derrida, as we shall soon see, is one of those who had a lot to say about deconstruction and decentredness.

Roland Barthes, however, is the most significant transition figure in the shift from structuralism to post-structuralism. We have already alluded to one of his works which is a structuralist study par excellence. His 1966 Essay, "The Structural Analysis of Narrative" is yet another. It is well-ordered, detailed, methodological and highly technical. In 1973, he wrote on the same theme, this time a full length book, *The Pleasure of the Text*.[16] This stands out, in comparison, as more disjointed and random. In fact, it is but a series of apparently disconnected remarks on narrative, arranged alphabetically: a typically post-structuralist manner of proceeding. Structuralism, while it summons us to question our way of structuring and categorizing reality seems, in the last analysis, is quite convinced that we can thereby attain a more reliable view of things. But post-structuralist writing is more emotive, less rational, often taking a more urgent and showy approach and likes to employ puns, allusions and other forms of word-play, for it is far more distrustful of reason and order.

In 1968, Barthes published *The Death of the Author*, which critics see as the hinge whereby he turned from structuralism to post-structuralism. His announcement of the death of the author was a rhetorical way of saying that the text is radically independent of its creator: what he intended to say, or the context within which he wrote – all this is irrelevant. The other side of the coin is the birth of the reader. In effect the text is something produced by the reader and, as it were, by language itself. Since the author is dead, there is no point in trying to interpret the text in terms of what "he" might have meant. There began the earlier phase of post-structuralism, characterised by "play", in which the reader has free vein to revel in endless "take-offs" from the text, as his whims and fancies may move him. Later developments in post-structuralism – especially (paradoxically, to some) with Derrida and "deconstruction" – more of discipline and less of hedonistic "free flights" come to be the order of the day, as we shall see.

3. Jacques Derrida (1930-2004)

Jacques Derrida, the man with whom "Deconstruction" has practically become identified, was born into a Jewish family, the son of Aime and Georgette Derrida, in El-Biar, Algiers. Interestingly enough, his family dwelling was entitled "The Garden" and appears to have functioned as a kind of Eden for him and his sister. This domestic oasis, however, "was framed by an environment where Jews were openly discriminated against – subjected to verbal and physical violence and prohibited from entering the legal or teaching professions."[17] No doubt his early experiences of marginalization and discrimination fired Jacques Derrida's resolve to show up the hollowness of the smug perspectives and "centres" from which people like him were being judged and found wanting.

Derrida went on to become one of the most controversial thinkers of his time. He held academic appointments in the Ecole Normale Supérieure, in Paris, and also at Yale University, at the University of California and at Cornell University. Situating himself within the tradition of Nietzsche, Husserl, Heidegger, Freud, A Saussure and Levinas, he mediated a critical encounter between two major philosophies in opposition: structuralism and phenomenology. His work calls into questions many of the traditional pre-suppositions of modern thought and his impact is far-reaching, influencing such diverse fields as literary criticism, cultural studies, sociology, anthropology, history, feminist and critical legal studies, besides philosophy.

The questions he addresses are of universal interest. He delves into the nature of language and human knowledge. He resurrects an age-old doubt that many had long come to think had been conclusively laid to rest: can we really know the truth about anything? He plumbs the meaning of Being (and, as a consequence, of God) and undermines the proud and overly confident claims of both philosophy and sciences to be a source of absolutely certain knowledge (*episteme*, in Greek). His writings are infuriatingly difficult and he has a penchant for puns, allusions and "play". One feels often tempted to throw up one hands in despair and cry out, "Is this man at all serious in what he is up to?" But don't be fooled by his antics. He is deadly serious and a scholar and creative thinker of no mean repute, to boot.

By the 1960s, Derrida had already achieved sufficient notoriety in France to be invited to America. At the Johns Hopkins University, in 1966, he gave a lecture entitled, "Structure, Sign and Play in the Discourse of the Human Sciences". This was quite an epoch-making lecture and caused quite a stir in the American literary and academic world. In it, he called for a radical re-reading of the basic philosophical texts that had become the mainstay of Western thought. It involved "reading the text against itself", or "against the grain", as Terry Eagleton put it.[18] This is to say that the deconstructionist tries to uncover the unconscious dimension of the text, which quite often is at variance with explicit and avowed intention. Far from being an irresponsible interpretation, where he tries to make the text say whatever he wants it to say, the interpreter makes a careful and well-disciplined study of the text. As a matter of fact, in 1967 – barely a year after his Johns Hopkins session – Derrida published *Of Grammatology*,[19] in which he interrupted his reading of Rousseau to reflect on what deconstruction is all about. Such a reading, he tells us, "must always aim at a certain relationship, unperceived by the writer, between what he commands and what he does not command of the patterns of language that he uses. [It] attempts to make the not-seen accessible to sight."[20]

Barbara Johnson, in her insightful study, *The Critical Difference,*[21] provides us with, perhaps, a fuller description. She says:

> Deconstruction is not synonymous with 'destruction'. It is, in fact, much closer to the original meaning of the word 'analysis', which etymologically means 'to undo'. ...The deconstruction of a text does not proceed by random doubt or arbitrary subversion, but by the careful teasing out of warring forces of signification within the text... [22]

Whereas traditional critics worked on the presumption that the text is actually a basic unity and all discordance and discontinuity is only apparent and should be overcome, the deconstructionist prefers to suspect that the opposite is the case. He is on the lookout for the recurrence of a tell-tale word or image, a chance allusion or an apparently innocuous aside and, through these, seeks to bring to the fore gaps, breaks and contradictions in the text. He is determined to show up the text as at war with itself, a house divided.

A good example of deconstruction a la Derrida is the presentation he gave in 1991, at a multidisciplinary, multinational conference at California University, on "Whither Marxism? Global Crises in International Perspective". The title of Derrida's paper was, "Specters of Marx". This gave him an opportunity to do some of his characteristic playful punning, here between "Ontology" and "Hauntology" (the two words, in French, are even less distinguishable, for the initial 'h' would be silent). In discussing his topic, Derrida sees himself as conducting a kind of *seance* (another French word which means both a session as also a meeting chaired by a 'medium' where he/she tries to call up spirito or spectres). He notes that the very first noun in the famous Communist Manifesto is his theme word, 'spectre': "A spectre is threatening; Europe, the spectre of Communism." And from the first verb in that opening sentence, he coins the term, 'hauntology". It implies a kind of ghost-science, for ghosts "haunt" us (and the word, in English as well as French, can also mean to frequent, as one may say of an alcoholic that he was "haunting the bars and the discoes of the city."

Thus he'll speak of two rival "ologies" who compete for international attention. Ontology concerns itself with beings and Being, about why there is something rather than nothing, about foundations and the basic ground of all reality. "Hauntology" would keep company with ghosts and spectres – non-beings, who traditionally occupy the space between being and non-being, life and death. Of course, given the fact that structuralism and post-structuralism have scant respect for ontology, he seems to be slyly suggesting that both are, in effect, busying themselves with non-beings, that the non-beings of "hauntology" are as much "beings" as those of ontology! There is quite a bit of "play" at work here...

Now, Derrida observes, keeping company with these spectres (and both "ologies" are busy with spectres) is a political act, because attending to being and non-being, life and death. This is done in the name of justice and responsibility is involved. So, "hauntology", 'ghost-science, the 'logic of the ghost' transcends the either/or binaries or dyads of life and death of 'to be' and 'not to be'

Derrida then goes on to point out that the "Western democracies," so jubilant about their health and so self-congratulatory at the apparent demise of Marxism, need to ask themselves just how full of life they really are. Could they have been in a worse state? Are they not more in a state of death, than life: torn by unemployment, overrun with exiles, crippled by the arms race, globalization is impoverishing the poorer nations and groups, the proliferation of mafia groups and drug barons who subvert whatever good any government can do and so on. And he asks, is this why all are so eager to exorcise the haunting spectre of Marxism – because we're not feeling too good ourselves and have unconscious fears about our own hour of death, being not too far off. On the other hand, the "spectre of Communism" is perhaps not so dead, not so much a spectre, a non-being after all. Perhaps the so-called liberal democracies are the real non-being, their freedom and democracy more a phantom than a reality. And so Derrida goes on to speak of the "New International", the new Marxist spirit that has been kept alive and is being continuously invigorated by some elements of the old Marxist spirit. Indeed, he finds two reasons why everyone should allow himself or herself to be possessed by the Marxist spectre, rather than seek to have it exorcised. First it urges us to close the gap between the ideals and the realities of the Western liberal democracies and, more radically, it is to question some of these very ideals itself. Derrida was no Marxist, but he was ready to let himself be seized by some elements of the Marxist spectre, distinguishing these from other ones, such as its history of totalitarian oppression, which is one element of the spectre which he'd be happy to exorcise and doesn't have to be part of a kind of packaged-deal spectre. He then makes a surprising comment – and does not clarify it: deconstruction would not have been able to have taken the form it now has if ours were a "pre-Marxist space"! Deconstruction, he clarifies, is, after all but a more radical form of Marxism.

Then Derrida gives his *coup de grace* to his whole "against the grain" reading of Marx. It is not only Europe that wants to do away with the spirit and spectre of Communism, he concludes: Marx too wanted it. After all, he wanted Communism to become a reality on earth – but then this would mean an end to its spectral existence – the spectre of Communism would be done away with!

Let's go back a moment, now, to the Johns Hopkins lecture. There Derrida presented a strong critique of structuralism, a critique that would have devastating effects on a host of other issues, in philosophy and out of it. A thing is to be understood by situating it within the context of the ever-widening concentric structures that surround it. So says structuralism. Fair enough. But, what struturalism has not realized is that structures are continually changing. Now each structure needs to have some sort of centre which controls and governs it. But if the structure is continually changing, the centre must always keep changing: it can't be a fixed point. The centre ends up by not being the centre; the centre is always elsewhere: the centre is not so much a place but a dialectic. In short, "we are living in a de-centred society"!

In his *Of Grammatology*, a fairly early work, as we have seen, Derrida followed up this insight by launching a broadside on what he calls the "metaphysics of presence" that has ever haunted Western thought. He has deliberately used the word "haunted" for, as we might suspect from our mention of "hauntology", this, too, is a spectre! The whole of Western thought, he observes, is a history of how speech has been favoured over writing and even the great de Saussure, in his *Course on General Linguistics* did so. Derrida dubs this bias *Logocentrism* (i.e. putting the 'logos', the written word at the centre of things). If words are a closed world, a system unto itself, logocentrism says it is the spoken word that is meant here, not the written word. Derrida indicates how written word/spoken word have been used as binaries or dyads, with the favored position given to speech, implying that the written word (the disfavoured one) lacks something that the preferred one has.

Now, what precisely does the spoken word have that the written one seems to lack? Precisely this sense of presence. When someone speaks to me, I cannot but be aware of his/her presence; when I read a letter or a book, its author, true, is "present" to me in a sense, but in a comparatively weaker way (in contrast to the person who stands before me and speaks to me). Since we are biased in favour of presence, writing is disfavoured. Now Derrida sets himself the task of deconstructing the metaphysics of presence to show that .it unconsciously favours writing: if this is not "reading a text against the grain", then nothing is.

In the first place, this bias in favour of speech, which is bound up with our penchant for presence, is all due to our predilection for "the transcendental signified". The signified we know from Saussure: it is the "mind image" (the concept), in contrast to the "sound image" (the spoken word). The transcendent signified refers to God or whatever ultimate, "beyond this world" entity (humanism, communism, capitalism) that we invoke as that which conserves and gives meaning to all that is in this world. Derrida is making an implicit deconstruction of the "transcendent signified" by reminding us that, inasmuch as it is seen as active in this world it is not so transcendent after all (of course, this objection is valid only if immanent/transcendent are understood to be "related opposites", binaries or dyads; but is not so if the two are conceived in a manner other than inside/outside).[23]

What Derrida does next is show to us that in spite of apparently all evidence to the contrary, meaning is actually more present in writing than in speaking (and, after all, it is the meaning of the message that is most crucial in communication). Well, just as we have seen that there is no internal link between the signifier (the word, or "sound-image") and the object (or "referrent"), so also there is no internal link either between the signifier and the signified. Only a naïve "metaphysics of presence" would believe that the signifier is the outer shell of which the signified is the kernel. There is no logical reason which binds the English sound "cow" to the concept of cow in my mind. As a matter of face any other sound could have been assigned to it (and this is precisely what other animals do). The signified is not really "present" within the signifier as even Saussure seemed to naïvely assume.

As for the various signifires, it is the play of difference between these various concepts that enables us to distinguish between them: the signifiers concerned have nothing to do with it at all! Now the play of difference in speaking (the "bow" sound being different from the "cow" or "how" sound) is also to be found in writing: a "b", "c" and "h", when written, mean nothing in themselves, but distinguish themselves from each other by the play of differences in the way they are written ("b" is not shaped like a "c"). Thus, speaking could as much be said to be a form of writing – though, traditionally, it has been put the other way round, with speaking being seen as more natural, normal and straightforward (which would mean that writing is somehow unnatural, abnormal and sneaky, to say the least). In other words, writing could just as much be made central to the whole issue, with speaking shoved to the margin. This would imply a rebellious and mischievous option for a metaphysics of absence: for meaning is, property speaking, absent to the signifier as to the written letters of the alphabet (it is in the signified).

This does not mean that Derrida merely wants to turn the tables: put writing at the centre and call it more natural, normal and straightforward and dump upon speaking all the unpleasant attributes of marginalisation. Instead he puts *both* terms, speaking and writing, under erasure (*sous rature* in French). Borrowing from Heidegger, he says that though we may be quite convinced that both terms 'speaking' and 'writing' are inadequate to describe the play of differences between them, yet, if we want to discuss them, we have no choice but to use them – for want of any alternative. Thus, following Heidegger's example with regard to the word 'being' (which he often wrote, 'crossed out' to warn us to be on our guard against its inadequacy: ~~being~~), so he began to write them as ~~speaking~~ and ~~writing~~. This allowed Derrida to eat his cake and have it too, as it were. Unable to avoid using these terms, he resigned himself to the inevitable, but put the 'cross-marks' over them to remind himself and us of their very inadequate nature for the job at hand (but there was no other alternative available in their place, so…)!

Finally, Derrida went on to invent an expression which would refer to the fact that both speaking and writing are forms of a more basic, non-existent form of writing, of which they were but a play of differences. He called this *arche-writing*! It doesn't exist as a thing, yet it makes writing and speaking possible!

A key quotation from *Of Grammatology* is, "There is nothing outside the text", and this is taken to exemplify his nihilism, a cosmism and whatnot. It is important that we re-situate this sentence within its proper context, otherwise we will end up misrepresenting its meaning after having torn it totally out of its sorting.

He is busy with interpreting, and commenting on, Rousseau's essay, "On the Origins of Language", when he suddenly pulls himself up short and starts reflecting on what he is doing. After all, an interpretation should not merely be a reproduction of what the author says, in his own words. Rather, it should be a "*supplément*" to it. Now *supplément* in French, means what it means in English: something which adds to, or completes, what was in another thing (an interpretation "*suppléments*" a text in the sense that it makes its meaning more clear). But it has also another sense in French, that of a replacement, in the sense that language re-places or stands in for reality. But, in what sense can language "stand in" for reality, given that language is something we inherit, with its own history, philosophy and rules (langue) already "built in", as it were? It seems that, in a sense, we don't express ourselves so much in words as in some aspect of language. As Derrida would put it:

> The writer writes *in* a language and *in* a logic, whose proper systems, laws and life, his discourse, by definition, cannot dominate absolutely. He uses them only by letting himself, after a fashion and up to a point, be governed by the system. And the reading must always aim at a certain relationship, unperceived by the writer, between what he commands and what he does not command of the patterns of the language that he uses. The relationship is not a certain quantitative distribution of shadow and light, of weakness or of force, but a signifying structure that critical reading *should* produce.[24]

Critical reading, then, should not aim at a faithful "reproduction of the text", as close an approximation of its "message", which the critic can then lay alongside the text (Derrida scornfully refers to this illusory and useless goals as "doubling the text": such a purpose is illusory and useless because it wrongly presupposes that there is some mysterious text that predates the one we are studying and which, purportedly, contains what the author wanted to say and which we are trying to reproduce or "double"!). If anything, the interpretation, rather than being reproductive or "doubling", should try to be deconstructive. in the sense explicated by Barbara Johnson.[25] It is at this point that Derrida makes the statement that commands our attention:

> Reading ... cannot legitimately transgress the toward something other than it ... or toward a signified outside the text, whose content could take place, could have taken place outside of language, that is to say, in the sense that we give here to that word, outside of writing in general. That is why the methodological considerations that we risk applying here to an example are closely dependent on general propositions that we have elaborated above, as regards the absence of the referent or the transcendental signified. There is nothing outside the text.[26]

Hopefully we have taken careful note of the context wherein this famous (mis)quote is enshrined. Derrida calls it "the axial proposition of this essay, that there is nothing outside the text",[27] and it should be clear enough that he is making a hermeneutical statement (when you interpret a text, do not take into consideration anything other than the text); he is not making the kind of metaphysical remark that many claim to have found there (nothing exists apart from the text, which is made up of words, words, words: a kind of "back to Plato" and his self-subsisting forms or ideas). Indeed, the very fact that Derrida says we should disregard any "signified outside the text", or "something other than it", implies – it seems to me – that there do exist things beyond the text, which are, strictly speaking, *not* the text!

Finally, he reiterates his point so as to stress what he would call "the metaphysics of absence" (a retort to the "metaphysics of presence!), which one is constrained to accept as soon as he recognizes that speaking could be viewed as a form of writing, besides the more traditional 'other-way-round' of viewing things. Nor does the 'metaphysics of absence' mean that this is the price we have to pay for making a 'preferential option' for writing over speaking! Both are in same boat: meaning is equally *not* inherent to either, is equally absent to both: in other words, "beyond and behind what one believes can be circumscribed as Rousseau's text, there has never been anything but writing ... what opens meaning and language is writing as the disappearance of natural presence."[28]

We have still not said anything about one of Derrida's key concepts, or more accurately, one of his key non-concepts. He has several, of course, but among his most favoured seems to be "différance" (and note the 'a' is not a typographical error!).

In the first place, these are more accurately described as 'non-concepts rather than 'concepts', because, once we 'conceptify' them, we forthwith invest them with attributes like stability and permanence and objectivity, all of which would fly in the face of what they would represent. So either we call them 'concepts' *sous rature*. or '~~concepts~~ or 'non-concepts'.

Now let's get back to *différance*, about which he devoted an entire lecture, in 1968, the year of radical revolt from which France has not yet fully recovered! Let's begin with the straightforward word, difference (French, *différance*), a linguistic term with which we are familiar, from Saussure's Course: the meanings of words derive, not from some kind of inherent, objective property resident within them, but insofar as they are elements in a system of differences (recall the syntagmatic chain, for one). Now, this brings us to another, very similar, word, to defer (meaning to delay, to postpone, to put off, as in, "The date of the exams was deferred because of the death of the prime minister."). Now, if meaning depends on one word's difference from other related words, then this would mean that its meaning would be forever be deferred or put off. Think of what happens in a dictionary, when you look up the meaning of a word. That word is defined in terms of other words. Now, to make sure of the meaning of the word you first looked up, you would have to check up on the meaning of those words used to explain it. But these would be defined in terms of yet other words, whose meaning you would also have to look up ... and on and on! Thus, the meaning of the original word would keep on being "deferred", put off! Now, with his predilection for punning and such verbal jugglery, Derrida combines both senses of "to differ" and "to defer" and coins *différance*. In the last analysis, *différance* embraces both meanings of difference and 'deference'. Not a very acceptable English word for 'delay'. Like the 'trick pictures' we saw of the glamorous young/ugly old woman and the candle-stand/two faces, which cannot be neatly pinned down into a strict either/or but keep up a continuous play of both, *différance* keeps shifting from one to another, always carrying with the one a "trace" of the other, such that at any one moment "a bit of both" is present!

In spoken English, it is possible to distinguish between difference and *différance*. In French, however, one cannot distinguish between difference and *différance* in their spoken forms: they are pronounced in exactly the same way. Only their written forms bring out their difference! This is one more reason to marginalise writing less and give it more prominence. And the point that Derrida wants to make is that the blank or suspense of meaning between difference and *différance* underlies all cases of differing (i.e. distinction) in writing. And it is this play of différance that is at work in all the "paired opposites" or binaries, like nature/nurture, raw/cooked, man/woman, etc.

The discussion of *différance* would serve us with an excellent transition point to discussing Derrida's – and deconstruction's – attitude to God! In the first place, différance, as many have pointed out, seems to function, for Derrida, as a kind of God-figure or, at least, a Being-figure (and both smack of being the "transcendental signifieds" that we have seen him so roundly attacking and rejecting). And the very fact that Derrida did caution his critics against viewing his *différance* as some kind of God of negative theology is, in itself, significant. Negative theology, we may recall, prefers to speak of God in terms of what God is not, rather than what God is: negative theology reminds us that, in the last analysis we know more about what God is not than what God is! Isn't this tantamount to accepting some kind of God, *sous rature*, ~~God~~? Not so, at least, not according to Jim Powell, a Derridean scholar, if ever there was one:

> (W)hen Derrida says that différance is neither a word nor a concept – and that there is no name for what différance is – it is not because différance is some supertranscendent, mystical essence in the Great Beyond. When Derrida says that différance is older than Being or God or any name of God, he is not making a religious statement, a theological statement, but a linguistic one. In order to say "God" you must use the word "God" in a system of differences. Difference is not some mystic, unnamable Being. Différance does not exist.[29]

In other words, by their very nature both différance and deconstruction make no statement about the existence or nature of God. However, were we to give some kind of name to God (Jesus, Allah, Brahman or whatnot), by that very act we would be seeking to give some kind of ground or hinge from which our Grand Myth or Meta Narrative would operate – and that would invite deconstruction. Deconstruction would always target any claim for a central, authoritarian, governing position. It would equally target an atheistic position that wants atheism to be a Grand Narrative or would purport to explain everything from that allegedly central position.

Be that as it may, it is difficult to deny some kind of religious overtone to a good deal of Derrida's writings and their implications and he, us we may except, doesn't make things easy for us when we push him into a corner. The nearest he came to giving us his personal credo is in his *Circumfession*, in 1993 (the coined word is, in itself, provocative enough): here he evokes his

> religion, about which nobody understands anything, any more than my mother, who asked other people a while ago, not daring to speak to me about it, if I believed in God. ... but she must have known that the constancy of God in my life is called by other names, so that I quite rightly pass for an atheist, the omnipresence to me of what I call God in my absolved private language being that neither of an eye-witness nor that of a voice doing anything than talking to me with-out saying anything.[30]

Here is equivocation if ever there was one. It contains enough for someone who'd be happy to "argue in both scales against either scale", like the Jesuits alluded to in Macbeth. "I quite rightly pass for an atheist", says Derrida, but that "pass" is what trips up interpretation, for it carries the meaning of "masquerade as", both in French and English – but it could also convey the sense of actually being a non-believer (the French *passe à juste titre* invites a "play" with both meanings, especially within its bewildering context of what amounts to not exactly a clear declaration of faith, but no straightforward affirmation of atheism either)jr. Yet, at Derrida's own admission, there appears to be some sort of admission of a 'God effect' (for want of a better phrase) in his life.

One can allude to another Derridean admission to the effect that he knows of mystics whose confession of faith "resembles a profession of atheism so as to be mistaken for it", though he makes no such claim over here. And what are we to make of Derrida himself confessing to us in a roundabout way (a "circumfession"?) that he employs a very "private language" purportedly in matters religious. In the first place, as everyone knows he never lost an opportunity to inveigh against anyone who advanced any pretensions about a private language of any kind. And, as if this admission weren't bad enough, he appears to be telling us that he was investing what looks suspiciously like his private version of a "transcendent signified" with a proper and personal name, an idiom unique to him alone. Then there's the apparently innocuous matter of the "absolved" language: what could that mean? After all, absolution can only come from another (or an Other) – one doesn't absolve oneself from anything. Which leads us to ask what he was being absolved from? Some list of omissions and commissions?

A deconstruction of Derrida's "circumfession" is too good a chance to miss. One could carry on the procedure with greater depth and at more length, of course. We hesitate to dub it "Derrida's credo", but then, isn't that we're judging him from the standards of the kind of credos we make, implying that there is a kind of "lack" in his version? Perhaps this is all we can expect of a deconstructionist's credo?

4. Jean-Francois Lyotard (1924-1998)

Born on August 10, 1924, at Versailles, not far from Paris, the city of the grandiose and magnificent palace of the "Sun-King", which is still a favourite haunt of tourists, Jean-Francois Lyotard was soon drawn to the Communist Party of Prance and became a dedicated an active member. In his youthful days as well as in his early academic career he made some forays into phenomenology but the main body of his writings at that time was solidly within the Marxist tradition. Not a few literary critics learnt from him to pen penetrating "Marxist criticisms" of Becket's *Waiting for Godot* and other avant-garde pieces of literature. He allied himself with a group called *Socialisme ou Barbarie* (Socialism or Barbarism), a radical Marxist group, which did not hesitate to critique the movement from within. He became more and more embittered with the closedness of the Party bosses to criticism and their authoritarianism and implicit claims of infallibility. Lyotard was in the frontline of the *évenements* of 1968, organising the student protests at Paris-Nanterre and, by the time the month of June had set in he had made a definitive break with his erstwhile Marxist faith and went on to become one of its most savage and ruthless critics. Anti-Marxism was soon the "in thing" in France, especially among the intelligentsia. "God is Dead and Marx is Dead and I'm not feeling too good Myself" (the title of a French best-seller) pretty well summed up the mood that would envelop French intellectuals for over a decade.

Soon Lyotard found himself ranked, with Derrida, among France's most illustrious exports. He was distinguished with professorships in the United States (at the University of California at Irvine) and back home: Paris VIII-Vincennes, St Dénis and co-founded the prestigious College International de Paris, along with his friend and colleague, Jacques Derrida.

In 1979, Québec University commissioned him to write *La condition postmoderne*. which was re-published in English translation, in 1984, as *The Postmodern Condition: A Report on Knowledge*.[31] This volume brought postmodernism as a concept and as a term into the centre of European intellectual debate and caught the attention of American intellectuals too (the British pooh-poohed postmodernism as not worthy of being dignified with the name of philosophy). His main thesis was that postmodernism is nothing more than an "incredulity towards metanarratives" (any theory or doctrine claiming to have universal validity, that is, that purported to provide an overall explanation of how and why things were happening in the world). Among such "Grand Narratives" were the myths of human progress and perfectibility ... and Communism! Thus postmodernity, in his hands, emerged as a deconstruction of one of the basic ideas of the Enlightenment, "the idea of a unitary end of history and of a subject" (which, it may be recalled, is precisely what the Marxist project had attempted to do). Lyotard was universally recognized as the most prominent spokesperson for postmodernism and he won over many scholars from various disciplines to the cause.

About the same time, also, he came under attack from many Marxist-inclined quarters, WHO saw him as a capitalist sympathizer who, for a fee or whatever, was doing their dirty work for them, slandering his former friends and co-revolutionaries. His Libidinal Economy had denounced all theory in general, and Marxism in particular, as a form of terror, but it soon became evident enough that he was not attacking Marxism from a capitalist perspective; rather, it was because he had launched a declaration of war on all totalities – which would include capitalism as much as Communism!

Grand narratives, by their authoritarianism and the tyrannical powers of coercion that they have amassed, become enemies of human freedom and put curbs on human creativity, even though they may have traced their birth to liberation movements of the people. On the other hand, he'd rather put his faith in "little narratives" (*petits récites*), by which marginalized groups and individuals can challenge the dominant patterns of development (fathered, primarily, by colonial powers, political and economic). The writings of Chinua Achebe, the Nigerian, especially his *Things Fall Apart* would be an excellent example of this. Repressive social systems can be gradually overthrown without having to take recourse to mass movements: individuals can contribute towards this by non-co-operation (Gandhian style) and by acting in alternative contrary and unpredictable ways. He coined the term "svelteness" to describe the way the individual can best challenge entrenched systems of cultural and social repression. It is a guerrilla-like attitude of flexible and creative response to pressures emanating from one's particular grand narrative – the ability to 'go to a ball in the evening and fight a war at dawn,' as Lyotard rather romantically puts it."[32]

The Postmodern Condition, however, does not stop with encouraging individual action against the totalitarian monster. It sets out a whole agenda that takes into account the Information Technology revolution of recent times. It is virulently critical of the dominant trends in globalisation, it calls for the destabilization of multinational corporations and institutions like the WTO and the IMF. Lyotard champions the cause of diversity over uniformity, of the individual over totalitarianism, of dissent and confrontation over coercion and enforcement. In the process he draws upon helpful developments to his vision from contemporary science, notably catastrophe theory and chaos theory and upholds the rights of "agnostics" and "paradox".

Lyotard's anti-authoritarianism and anti-foundationalism are highlighted in the way he depicts the legitimation of power and authority in *The Postmodern Condition*. Contrary to the popular conviction, he points out, authority justifies itself not so much by proofs or by the unveiling of the truth but by manipulation of power, which they use to, for instance, write history to suit their own ends (history is written by the conquerors and depicts the colonizers who are doing a favour to the "natives", portrayed as immoral, irreligious and uncultured barbarians whom the "Great White Colonial Mother Country" brings morality, civilization and culture). The multi-national corporations of today, he argues, under the guise of foreign aid and providing employment to Third World people, actually further exploit and impoverish them in order to make unlimited profits at little or no expense to themselves (and every expense to the poorer nations who cannot fight back or resist).

A common objection raised against Lyotard's all-out war on grand narratives, so as to secure justice for the underdog, is whether we can explore and realise the 'fair and free' society he envisages without any absolute criteria to guide us. In response to this line of attack, Lyotard agreed to a seven-day exchange on this theme with Jean-Loup Thébaud, editor of *Esprit*. This resulted in *Au Juste* (English version, *Just Gaming*) in which he seems to have maintained a rather consistent position. Even though absolute criteria are to be rejected, it is still possible to make judgments on what is going on in the international scene. This is because judgment becomes an aesthetic (not an epistemological!) undertaking, whereby one respects differences.

Again, in *Le différend* he further elaborates his understanding of judgment in the various phases of a dispute. As is probably obvious, *Le différend* literally means 'the different' and here he indulges in a lengthy conversational exchange with the entire history of western thought, through sporadic sections, interspaced with notes that are as long as whole chapters. Thus, in his hands, philosophy becomes more a style-of-thinking than a presentation of the conclusions of one's critical thinking.

In his final works, Lyotard sought to integrate into his manner of philosophising a host of other disciplines and styles of expression. In *Pérégrinations* (*Ramblings*) he opened himself to poetic concerns and added phrases like pagan aesthetic and parology to his vocabulary. Time may prove that his philosophico-poetics will be his most enduring legacy. His last two writings, *Moralités Postmodernes* (*Postmodern Moralities*) and *Signé Malraux* (*Signed Malraux*) were rendered into English after his death (on April 21, 1998, at Paris): in them he brought together even more diverse narrative forms, such as biography, autobiography, fiction and literary theory. He gave us a fine example of postmodern respect for diversity! Various genres are presented alongside each other without any one form trying to impose its approach on all this heterogeneity.

Lyotard's weakness is perhaps his strength. For he ends up arguing (with approval) that we live in a highly fragmented universe. True to his anti-totality (and anti-foundationalist) bias, he holds that we can but bear witness to *le différend* (unresolved conflicts) that set off one genre from another. *Within* a particular genre, or literary form, judgments can be made, he tells us (though we have to admit that he's rather vague as to how exactly this is to be done), but certainly not *across* genres. Doing this, and doing it glibly, is a particular characteristic of politics which, as he never wearies of reminding us, is notoriously intolerant of *différends* and would like all minority groups and dissidents to be reined in and swallowed up by the dominant meta-narrative, capitalism, Roman Catholicism, globalisation, Hindutva or whatever. The responsibility of the philosopher is to preserve *differénds* and resist all national-political attempts to resolve the unresolvable and brainwashing us into thinking either that we actually are, or should be, saying the same thing! If this is a call to radical politics, and I think it decidedly is, Lyotard does little or nothing to present a cogent plan of campaign. At most he seems to be calling for a conversion of mind and heart and that sort of appeal would hardly inspire leftist activists!

He refuses, as we have seen, any absolute criteria of judgment and, at the practical level seems to endorse a rather pragmatic method of approach: act in favour of what would serve the interest of the little narrative (*petit récit*) in its conflict with the grand narrative. This is where he advocates what he calls 'paganism', judging without any criteria apart from (presumably), the needs of the particular *petit récit* applying at the time. This paganism is very appealing, but Lyotard skirts a very obvious question: what is to be done when the entrenched power refuses to play by any rules and cracks down on the minorities (as it often and usually does)? Many on the left, quite justifiably I think, accuse Lyotard of a certain naïvety, impracticality and practical irrelevance in what he says.

There is no doubt that *The Postmodern Condition* has had considerable impact on the cultural debate over the last decade or so and has provided a much-needed shot-in-the-arm for many flagging protest movements and minority groups. It can even be seen as a prophetic work, seeing what came to pass in the Soviet Union and elsewhere. On the other hand, he seems to have a very romantic view of the capacities of the little narrative to assert itself and challenge the grand narratives, though he has highlighted very well the inherent weaknesses of the dominant powers that be. History seems to be proving, however, that institutional power is not so vulnerable to the upsets that the *petits récits* can muster: multinationals have emerged unscathed from the pinprick attacks of the little narratives. Still, his views have had an undeniable impact on liberative struggles and he has added plenty of matter for reflection to the libertarian debates of our time.

5. Michel Foucault (1926-1984)

Michel Foucault, born in Poitiers (where the French lost a decisive battle to the English some centuries back), on October 15, 1926, is arguably one of the most versatile and influential of postmodernist thinkers. His ideas have impacted on psychiatry, history, linguistics, literary analysis, science, the history of ideas, criminology, jurisprudence and ethics. His work, as well as his election to the prestigious Collège de France was a symptom and sign of the breakdown in the traditional perception of the role of knowledge in social formation in his country!

You could say that his wide field of study was held together by his consuming interest in how knowledge and power work together. In fact, his academic life could be seen as a prolonged reflection on the now well-worn adage, 'Knowledge is Power'. He took this saying, as it were, and dismantled it, analysed it and put it back together. He was particularly interested in the knowledge *of* human beings and in the power that acts *on* human beings.

Among the basic questions he drew from this are the following: How did 'man' come to know himself? What was the Enlightenment really about – knowledge or power? What drove modern European man to make knowledge into power, submitting every object or person to the domineering straitjacket of what 'he' called 'objectivity'?

Suppose we grant the statement that knowledge *is* power but, like the postmodernists, deny that we have any knowledge of absolute truth. In that case, what would knowledge mean? Perhaps it would be no more than what a group of people get together and decide is true. Well, for Foucault, the 'might' in the other proverb, 'Might is Right' is not so very different from the 'power' in 'Knowledge is Power'. In the former case, physical force, in the latter mental force, is exerted by a very powerful minority, who are thereby able to impose their idea of what is right or true, on the hapless and helpless weak minority. And that is Foucault's thesis in a nutshell!

He had been named Paul-Michel, but later decided that he'd rather be Michel than Paul. Already at the age of four he was sitting in the prestigious Lycée Henri IV, not because he was something of a child prodigy, but because he could not bear being separated from his elder sister. So, there he sat quietly in the back, a well-behaved and obedient little chap, playing with his crayons and, perhaps, listening in occasionally to the lessons. When he did enrol there, two years later, he began to distinguish himself in his work from an early age and clearly seemed to have enjoyed his schooldays.

When he was thirteen, it was felt that the time had come for him to face up to a more demanding academic environment and so he was packed off to the Jesuit-run Collège Saint-Stanislaus. Too young to become a war hero (France was to fall before the German advance, soon later), he nevertheless helped his classmates to steal wood from the Nazis, so as to heat their school. He gave a good account of himself at the Collège, but always stood second to his close friend, Paul Rivière. At the end of the war he was to remark that he found it much easier to survive the demanding war years than the extremely rigorous pressures of the French school system, which some have compared to the strenuous discipline of preparing for the Olympics. At 17, he had a major row with his father when he told the latter in no uncertain terms that he had no intention of following in his footsteps (nor those of his grandfather, either) by becoming a surgeon. His father was quite upset as he had great plans for his gifted son, who had won fourth place in all of France, from those competing for admission to the famed Ecole Normale Supérieure of Paris, the country's most exclusive and intellectually demanding college-level school.

In 1950, along with most of his friends, he joined the Communist Party but quit in 1955 (about the time of Stalin's death), having been more and more disillusioned by the crackdowns and terror tactics that were becoming commonplace in the Soviet Union. Soon after, he left for Sweden, where he had secured a post as French teacher at Upsala. There he came across, and immersed himself in a library of medical works from the sixteenth to the twentieth centuries. Thence he gathered most of the material he would use in his later writings on the history of the development of hospitals in general and of the 'insane' and other 'abnormal' persons.

There is little doubt that his sexual preferences influenced his major interests. Openly gay within his own circle, he never really 'came out of the closet' to the public at large. He was quite active in gay politics, but never strident about it. When he died, in 1984, his family, at first, refused to admit that he had died of AIDS. Actually, it is debatable whether he knew he had the dreaded sickness at all: in the early eighties, knowledge of AIDS at that time was not properly spelt out. Had his doctors told him, he was dying of it, he would have probably dismissed the very idea as nonsense and a homophobic prejudice that be just had to be smitten with 'the gay plague', given his lifestyle. Whether he knew he had it or not, he never mentioned it to his friends and for many in the gay community, he thereby lost his chance to have made an important political point.

Foucault's intellectual output was, as we have said, the fruit of his protracted meditation on the well-worn adage that 'Knowledge is Power'. The question that fascinated him was the mechanics of this power-acquisition. How does an individual (or a group) get people to agree to his/their truth as *the* truth? After all, the one who gets the most people to accept 'his' truth (the choice of the masculine pronoun is deliberate!) as 'the' truth has power!

He recognised that sometimes there is an overt and explicit connection between knowledge and power, as when a child is spanked to 'teach him a lesson.' Most often this is communicated through language. As soon as a child learns to speak, he is told things like, 'Take good care of your Mummy, Son.' 'Daddy's going to work!' Thus his childish brain is already making the association: 'Daddy: work', 'Mummy: home'. In effect, Foucault was giving Socrates' oft quoted, "Know Thyself!" a more specific thrust: discover how our hunger for the accumulation of power creates various techniques and strategies for its fulfilment: 'rituals of exclusion' (about which, more below!), selection, distortion, repression and so on.

In 1961, he published his thesis, a 600-page long study, entitled *Folie et Déraison* (English title: *Madness and Civilisation*) – two more volumes were added and both were published in 1984. His first provocative remark is that what we call 'madness' is not a kind of common malady shared by certain people in various ways (for there's so much variation in their symptoms – from dangerous aggressivity to absolute docility and passivity – that, unless you have been brainwashed into tarring them all with the same brush, you wouldn't lump them together in the same group). Foucault's hypothesis is that we *need* to exclude some people from society, to lock them up and keep them out of sight. 'Madness' is just the name we give to the class of people we decide should be 'put away'. Eventually, as we will see, this will be broadened to include criminals and the sick (not only those with contagious diseases). For some reason we *have to* segregate certain people from our conscious gaze.

Foucault then proceeds on a historical study as to which kinds of people were targeted for the 'lockup', down the ages. Starting with the Middle Ages (from which period, data begins to be available), we note that everybody wanted to isolate and keep out of sight those afflicted with leprosy (quite common, then) – people who not only suffered from a disease taken to be contagious, but were also unpleasant to look at. Then, suddenly, with the fourteenth century (and development of hygiene?) leprosy was on the decline and then practically disappeared in Europe. If everyone was happy about that they wondered what to do with the now empty lockups, the leprosaria. For a while they let these remain unoccupied.

Attention then shifted to a group that, until then, had been accepted within society and even taken care of by their families, the 'insane'. Either because people found them embarrassing to have around, or too time-consuming or beyond their capacity to handle, they invented the solution of 'The Ship of Fools'. All 'madmen' were herded together and, by order of the State (even if their families protested), were loaded on to a ship and set sail down a river, wandering from one port-town to another, never allowed to disembark, hastily expelled from the harbour or docks or jetty (invariably with a payment to the captain to ferry them ever on, ever elsewhere). By this time, Foucault tells us, there had developed a 'cultural fascination with madness': on the one hand, it had to be put out of sight, on the other hand, people derived some kind of morbid fulfillment by having opportunities for a (safe!) glance at it. All this is expressed in writings like Erasmus' *In Praise of Folly* (1509) and the plays of Shakespeare where jesters and madmen are presented as having access to a higher wisdom than that of us 'normal' people: witness, for example, the 'home truths' that the temporarily mad sovereign hears and delivers in *King Lear* (1605). Truly, as Hamlet had put it, "There's method in madness"!

Then came the seventeenth century, the Age of Incarceration or of the Great Confinement. At the slightest excuse, people were arrested and summarily locked up. Criminals, of course, had to be imprisoned (but even people guilty of minor infractions were locked up). The insane were also put behind bars (*not* in asylums, but in jails!) and just about anyone who acted strangely or a little bit differently from everyone else – and this included epileptics – met the same fate. The unemployed were also rounded up and beggars were told to get jobs or be prison-fodder, too. Some of the old leprosaria were reserved for the sick who, until then, lived among their families and were treated by them. Orphans, widows – these, too, were fair game for confinement (along with the old)!

By the seventeenth and eighteenth centuries more humane suggestions were made (if not always followed) for the incarceration of people (about 1% of the total population of Paris, for one example, was locked up, on some pretext or other), except for the 'madmen'. Madness was considered to be particularly shameful and so had to be hidden from the sight of respectable people.

It is illuminating (to say the least), to ask ourselves how those times saw madness. What did they think it consisted of? What made people go mad? Well, they primarily thought of it as a physical disease (nothing to do with the mind). It was all due to hysteria, they said, and they went on to define hysteria as 'having convulsions for no apparent cause'. Now hysteria comes from the Greek word for a womb;[33] it was believed that madness was caused by the fact that a woman's uterus (womb) could become dislodged from its normal position and wander about the body (carrying its precious cargo with it) and this would result in the child being born with hysteria, which would lead to madness. This idea was gradually given up, but notice how woman is once again made the scapegoat: madness is all the mother's fault, it's all because something wasn't right within her! What Foucault missed in his brilliant historical analysis was that this *cherchez la femme* approach was typical of the unfair treatment doled out to women at that time: right up till the nineteenth century, among the people who were destined for the lock up, were women who'd had sex with men they weren't supposed to (their 'partners-in-crime', if that's the right phrase, of course, went scot-free!).

By the close of the eighteenth century, it became clear that physical treatment alone would not cure madness. But this was not yet the beginning of psychological treatment, not by a long chalk. It was believed that body, soul and mind were so inter-related that what affected one would touch up upon the other two.

Then, quite unexpectedly there came the French Revolution (unexpectedly, as far as treatment of the insane was concerned). Languishing in prison, shortly before the évenemants of 1789, had been two upper-class libertines (sex-defaulters also had to be locked away, lest their sight offend the respectable folk). One was the Marquis de Sade, father of sadism, a truly immoral and psychologically sick individual. He was soon let out of jail whereas the other, Mirabeau, much less of an immoral person and assuredly not psychologically sick – soon to be the hero of the Revolution – was left to rot in jail, until the storming of the Bastille set him free. This fact alone symbolised, for the revolutionaries, what was wrong with the world. Once released from prison, Mirabeau went on to become one of the major leaders of the people in their revolt against the monarchy, the church and the aristocracy. Now it was these who would fill the lockups!

Meanwhile the plight of 'the mad' was somewhat different. After the Revolution, they were supposed to be released from prison (mainly because the other inmates felt it was too humiliating to be cooped up with the insane) and put into special hospitals. But these 'special hospitals' didn't exist, so they were sent home to their families. Very soon, their families wanted to get rid of them, because it was felt, rightly or wrongly, that it was too troublesome to take care of them. So they went back into prisons, except that this time, the madmen and the criminals were carefully segregated.

About this time there surfaced two great myths of 'benefactors of the mad', men who were seen as great humanisers in the treatment of insanity. There was Philippe Pinel who, during the Revolution, threw open the prisons and let the madmen out. He is reported to have declared, "I am convinced that these madmen are so intractable because they have been deprived of fresh air and liberty." Thus the insane had their own revolution and their own liberator. And then there was Samuel Tuke, a gentle Quaker, who set up a rural retreat for the mad. They purportedly lived there in idyllic harmony and in a familial atmosphere.

The harsh reality was somewhat different. To begin with Tuke and his farm-family: it was a family all right, but the mad were treated as no better than indisciplined children who had to learn – the hard way, if need be to accept the authority of their father, Tuke himself. He decided what was good for them. For instance, they had to be taught religion, whether they liked it or not. And they were forced to be productive: *Arbeit macht frei [Hard Labour Makes One Free]*, as it would be proclaimed elsewhere, barely 150 years later.[34] And if the naughty children rebelled or disobeyed, why the chains were put back until one learned to behave. In other words, the mad were taught their madness was their responsibility. Other people were watching your every move, so you better watch yourself, control yourself as per the directives of Big Daddy, or else… The great 'ritual of control' for Tuke's therapy was the specially organised, carefully watched tea party. Each inmate was assigned the role of a visitor from afar and each had to conduct himself with due decorum and politeness, while their guards and mentors observed them carefully to catch the slightest sign of unusual or individualistic behaviour. Observation and control were everything in Tuke's formula.

Pinel's was no better. His idea was to mete out punishments of the most cruel and embarrassing kind to all who transgressed what he laid down as the laws of acceptable conduct. Cold showers and the straitjacket were remorselessly employed (plus a few other methods not really mentionable in polite society), until the mad person began to display signs of remorse and thereafter provide his or her own inner discipline.

Finally, in order to give more credit to what they were attempting, both Tuke and Pinel hired doctors to visit their institutions. Such men were taken for granted as noble and wise figures and soon they took over from the two great 'liberators of the mad' their role as fathers of their patients. However, these doctors were not in the least bit qualified to treat patients of this kind but that scarcely mattered: to the mad, and to society at large in those days, the doctor seemed an omniscient, divine figure with quasi-magical power and the doctor basked in this aura, even though he might have feebly protested that he was but a man and his skill was purely scientific.

All this climaxed with the arrival of Papa Freud, with whom Foucault closes his 600-page study. Freud epitomised the conviction that the doctor knows best, that the patient must submit to his diagnosis and régime of treatment and cure. Foucault, who had had his own stint with a 'shrink' wasn't at all convinced about all this. But, on this note, he ended volume I: 600 pages was enough for the moment!

Foucault was already flushed (and horrified?) by what he had discovered: the lengths that some people would go in order to fulfil what he was convinced was a deep-seated yearning in all of us: the passion to control, dominate, brainwash, indoctrinate and watch each other. In the old days, kings and sorcerers decided the fate of people. Today, these roles are usurped by many more people: parents, educators, the police, criminologists, the clergy, psychiatrists, doctors… the list is endless. Formerly various disciplinary organisations were drafted in to help with the job: schools, churches, hospitals, asylums, jails… Nowadays, we can fall back on far more efficient techniques of control: audio video surveillance, identity checks, passwords, cybernetic implants, electronic bracelets, mood-control and memory-control drugs…

In 1963, *The Birth of the Clinic* saw the light of day (English translation, 1973). Its sub-title was "The Archaeology of the Medical Gaze". That last word will become a kind of tocsin that summons us to battle against the invasion of our privacy by the powers that be. "This book", Foucault informs us in the opening pages, "is about space, about language and about death; it is about the act of seeing, the gaze." After all, what is a patient but a thing to be gazed at by the professional eye of the doctor and the nervous, amateur eye of the medical student, under the critical and judgmental gaze of, once again, the doctor? The patient must remain silent and passive while the others gaze on him/her and discuss among themselves what their gaze has revealed to them alone. The notion of a hospital as a place where patients are treated and doctors are trained, at one and the same time, was seen by Foucault, once again, as the creation of the French Revolution.

Now, the French Revolution had two great, idealistic medical dreams. First, there would be a nationalised, quasi-religious order of doctors, who would zealously dedicate themselves to the care of the body, with the same spirit that once priests had devoted themselves to the care of their parishioners' souls. Secondly, they envisioned a transformed society in which there would be no more sickness and no more people needing medical care at all. After all, they rationalised, poor people got sick because of their miserable living conditions, but the Revolution had solved all this. As for the rich, their diseases were but the effect of their dissipated lives and the Revolution had put an end to this, too. After the Revolution, then, hospitals were closed down: they were seen as a waste of good money and, it was argued, people would get better and more loving care at home. As for the universities, these were the bastions of the élite, so they had to be done away with. Funds for hospitals and academic purposes needed to be put to alternative, better use… or were simply embezzled.

However, in spite of all the rationalising, people still got sick and often tender, loving care at home wasn't enough to help them. Besides, there were wars going on and soldiers were getting wounded. So hastily medical officers were recruited, trained and let loose upon the pain-wracked and disabled warriors. After the war, when demobilization set in, these 'doctors' began to practise in civilian life and often did far more harm than good to their patients. University trained doctors began to teach students in secret, until it was clear that a more drastic solution was required and the whole system had to be rebuilt from scratch. Hospitals were constructed, invariably close to, or connected with, universities.

Thus, emerged the 'clinic set-up', as Foucault sees it. Teaching is, here, united with practice. Doctors cannot get licensed unless they have done a stint in the clinic. The Professor of Medicine, followed by his coterie of nervous students, sometimes tests them by questioning them, or makes his diagnoses and decides treatment. If he makes a mistake – which cannot be helped for we are all fallible – his students get to know it (which is embarrassing to him) and the patient has to pay the price but, at least, he knows that the onward march of the medical science will profit from his loss. Gradually, hospitals become more specialised. Patients with similar complaints are segregated into separate hospitals or separate wards in the same hospital. The more unusual and complicated diseases are studied more intently. It is the disease, not the patient who is important or interesting. Above all these presides the all-knowing doctor with his all-powerful eye, which he turns for a brief moment on each patient as he walks from one bed to another, followed by his alert, attentive and timid students. A kind of active vision, which Foucault epitomises as 'the gaze' is elevated into great importance in medicine. The doctor's perception is all-important; an unobservant doctor is a contradiction in terms. Where earlier definitions might have stressed a physician's actions, a good doctor is now one who sees all:

> Over all these endeavours on the part of clinical thought to define its methods and scientific norms hovers the great myth of a pure Gaze that would be pure language: a speaking eye. It would scan the entire hospital field, taking in and gathering together each of the singular events that occurred within it; and, as it saw, it saw ever more and more clearly, it would be turned into speech that states and teaches…[35]

But this all-seeing eye is not quite able to understand the complexity of the human phenomenon: too much is still hidden from it – the inner makeup of the body, with its complex of organs, arteries, bones and what not. These must not be allowed to escape the ravings and the plumbings of the would-be omniscient eye. So 'opening up corpses' suddenly took on a new significance. It had been going on for some time, but now it is to be brought under the gaze. It is as if nothing that makes up the human person should be granted asylum or sanctuary from its relentless quest.

Thus, imperceptibly (according to Foucault, at any rate), death and disease become crucial to throwing light on life: in effect, death shifts from being the lack of life, to its culmination. After all, it is in and through death that the gaze perfects its knowledge of the human person.

Foucault's next publication flung down the glove, as it were, in direct challenge to Sartre's brand of humanism. This is evident from the very title he chose for his book, in the original French. Sartre had entitled his autobiography, *Words*, Foucault presented himself as post-Sartrean by bringing out a work called, *Words and Things* (the English title is *The Order of Things*). The sub-title was "An Archaeology of the Human Sciences" and, in it, Foucault contested the penchant from the eighteenth century onwards for grouping all disciplines around the human person. He remarks, tongue in cheek, "Before the eighteenth century, man did not exist." What he was underlining, of course, was the centrality given to man (he overlooked the masculinity of the word) in modernism. But, as Foucault reminded us, "Man is neither the oldest nor the most constant problem that has been posed for human knowledge."[36] After all, the pre-Socratics (who, in the opinion of Nietzsche and Heidegger, represented the real 'Golden Age' of western thought), had focused attention on the meaning of 'being' and the quest for the archē – that primeval stuff out of which all things were made – than on the issue of man! Foucault's questioning of this naïve putting way of man at the centre of all things was a typical postmodernist approach which already put Sartrean humanism into doubt. But that was not all.

He did agree with Sartre that meaning is something that we construct: there is no transcendent meaning inherent in the world, independent of the human person. But where he felt that Sartre was pretty naïve was in the latter existentialist conviction that we can rise above the social conditioning that constructs us, so as to freely 'make meaning': this was what Foucault denied, as, indeed, all structuralists and post-structuralists had done! In other words, control and indoctrination surrounds us on every side. Sartre was so simplistic: man, not just God, was dead! The archaeology of the human sciences, which goes to join the archaeology of the medical gaze, confirms this. Other 'archaeologies' would follow and these would only present his case more forcefully. There was *The Archaeology of Knowledge* (1969) and *Discipline and Punish* (1975), not to mention the three volumes of his *History of Sexuality* (Volume I came out in 1976 and the other two in 1984).

Discipline and Punish presented the grand climax of techniques of control, the 'panopticum', envisioned by the British utilitarian philosopher, Jeremy Bentham (1748-1832). What Bentham dreamt of, as the ideal way to make everybody behave, is what Foucault sees the world as heading towards and he doesn't think it is something to rejoice about.

> The idea is that every person is isolated in a small room, where all may be observed at all times by a single person in the central tower. The building would be lit around the perimeter, so that each person could be clearly seen by the central observer, but each inmate would see neither the observer nor any other inmate. Bentham envisioned the same basic concept for factories, schools, barracks, hospitals, madhouses and especially, prisons.[37]

An elaborate and carefully graded system of punishments would be worked out and meted out proportionate to the offences one was caught in the act of committing. The 'panopticum' is the grand fulfillment of our deep, inborn desire to control, discipline and exercise over each other that power which arises from knowledge – knowledge of everyone else's most (allegedly!) secret actions. Sexual mores were but another way of appeasing that innermost drive of man (once again, Foucault seems to ignore the masculinity of the word). Only one area still seems to escape the 'panopticum': human thoughts. Religious authorities and petty dictators have tried to control that, too. With the advent of computers, electronic implants and 'truth drugs' maybe this will also become possible – unless we decide to do something about it all!

6. Jean Baudrillard (1929-2007)

The social theorist, Jean Baudrillard, was born at Reims in 1929. He was to teach sociology at Paris-Nanterre from 1966 onwards. The May 1968 uprising had its impact on him, as on all his colleagues and slowly weaned him away from his stumbling attempts to make Marxism credible to the public in general and the student world in particular, even though it stubbornly held aloof from recent developments in arts, mass communications, social organisations, economics and class relations. His publication of *Simulations*, in 1961 (English translation, 1983) marks his entry into the hurly-burly of postmodernism. Nowadays he is considered more a populariser of the fad, a kind of eclectic producer of 'coffee-table' format books on postmodernism, recommended for those who need to make intelligent noises at cocktail party circuits. *America*[38] and *Cool Memories*[39] are cases in point.

Until the 1960s he was content to be a kind-of left-revolutionary radical, translating Brecht[40] and avant-garde writers of his ilk into French. He had been greatly inspired by his own sociology teacher, Henry Lefebvre, into initiating a 'Marxist-inspired critique of everyday life'. In the seventies, he stands out as still a Marxist, but a radical one, for he would stress the role of culture in the formation of capitalist ideology (conventional Marxists would prefer to speak about the role of economic in all this). Like Barthes, he seems to have been seized with a special interest in consumerism and the social attitudes and behaviour that it enkindled. He gradually became more and more critical of the monolithic Communist Party of France, with its proud aloofness from the epochal socio-technological developments of the age. He became increasingly fascinated with the impact of cybernetics on society and, tongue in cheek, described it as a 'cyberblitz'! No longer could Marxism maintain that class conflict was creating social order: that role had now been usurped by *simulacra* confirmed, consolidated and well-focused by information technology. These 'simulacra', as we shall see, are reproductions of events, captured as images by the media and which – more than the actual events they represented – were constituting (in more senses than one) the 'real' world of ours, After all, in the postmodern era, cybernetic-generated simulation models decide what is 'real' for us and the human person has become but a 'switching centre for all the networks of influence' that technology is able to spawn.

If his *For a Critique of the Political Economy of the Sign* (1972) rejects the traditional Marxist notion of 'use value', he wasn't very successful in coming out with an alternative model to propose in its place. His full-fledged rejection of Marxism is evident in *The Mirror of Production* (1973) and *Forget Foucault* (1977) where he accuses him of basing itself on a naïve 'epistemological mirror of objective reality'!

He is about the only postmodernist who can claim to have inspired – albeit, in spite of himself – a whole new art form, 'situationism'. Its most illustrious representative was Guy Delord (1931-1994) and the movement favoured a distinctive approach to graphic design, using political slogans and doctored images from the popular press and from advertisements. However, he didn't seem to have much appreciation for its productions!

Something of a prima donna, he loves to play to the gallery and delights in making outrageous, offensive and exaggerated remarks, such as, "Reality no longer exists" or "The year 2000 will not take place!" or "The Gulf War did not take place". If this kind of brash, deliberately provocative and ironic remarks shocked his fellow-countrymen and other Europeans (to his immense joy), they certainly endeared him to American pop academics and artists. Thus, Douglas Kellner hailed him as the 'Walt Disney of contemporary metaphysics."[41]

In a 1993 essay, "Simulacra and Simulations" he evokes a past era of 'fullness': this was when a sign had a quasi-sacramental status and revealed an invisible inner depth or reality. Now, however, Baudrillard is convinced, times have changed: signs are but signs of other signs and there is no underlying reality behind or below them. We have now an age of 'emptiness'. Where signs had once allegedly been representations (they stood for a deeper, underlying 'reality'), they are now but 'simulations' (mirages, appearances that point to, or manifest, no basic, deep down reality at all) and the whole system is but a 'simulacrum'. Typical of this is that well known US creation, Disneyland! One could say that it incarnates all the USA's values, canonising them, as it were, in comic-strip form. Embalmed and taxidermised they are offered to you, a tribute and panegyric to the American way of life, an idealisation of the American reality. After a while, however, we begin to realise that Disneyland *is* America, for 'the great American dream' and 'the American way of life' exist only in Disneyland and nowhere else. The ghettoes, the spiralling violence and narcotic addiction among its youth (and children!), the scandalous disparity between the rich and the poor, the brutal and alienating architecture, the rabid consumerism and gross self-centred ideology – all these repugnant traits of America are sought to be covered over. Disneyland is then trotted out to impress upon us that the 'real' America is this. And thereby it is used to distract us from the ugly face of the US that no one is supposed to notice. Thus, Disneyland has the effect of "concealing the fact that the real is no longer real, and thus of saving the reality principle."[42] In other words, postmodernism ends up destroying the distinction between what is real and what is simulated or pretended. There is a 'loss of the real' in favour of the 'hyper-real' (Disneyland is presented, in the last analysis, as more real than the 'real' America, itself!)...

This is quite a strong criticism and a 'no-holds-barred' attack on American culture, if ever there was one. But Baudrillard never seems to be quite sure of his stance. He will soon switch on to an exuberant celebration of that superpower's 'banality', in a nigh-lyrical vein that Walt Whitman himself could hardly rival! After all, it was his laudatory words on how the demolition of skyscrapers could constitute a marvellous new art form in itself that led to the launching of 'situationism'.

Many Marxists disgustedly and bitterly remark, that this former critique of capitalism consumerism has sold himself lock, stock and barrel to his erstwhile foe. To many Europeans, he seems to be uncritically accepting – and even rejoicing in – America's obliteration of all those last vestiges of continental mores: value-consciousness, aesthetic depth, the dignity of the human person. Of late he appears to becoming more of a spectator and less and less of a critical thinker. Indeed, he appears to hold up America as the model of the hyper-real future to which all should aim, one where reality and simulation have become fused into one.

But then, just as we were getting used to this blind endorsement of hyperrealism, he suddenly assumes what looks like a Buddhist mask. He startles us by elevating the desert as the new exemplar which all of us must try to realise in our personal lives. In the twinkling of an eye, we are summoned from the heights of flagrant consumerism to the simplicity and asceticism of Zen Buddhism: 'desertification' becomes the new rousing cry. The self must be stripped down to its basic minimum and the grasping mentality, so assiduously and uncritically cultivated until now, has to be jettisoned. Our goal must be, 'No desire: the desert!'

Cool Memories consolidates and deepens this trend towards a kind of post-aesthetic sensibility, where all value-judgment is to be suspended. He prattles: "There is a charm and a particular freedom about letting just anything come along" and it looks as if he is advocating an aimless, passive drifting amid the massively disorienting, techno culture. This apoliticism is probably the worst aspect of his abject surrender to American capitalism that renders him totally irrelevant for the Third World scene in general, and for India in particular.

One gets the impression that when the pressure of international criticism and outrage forced him to make at least some revolutionary-sounding noises, he did so in an idiom calculated to provoke yet another section of his interlocutors, the feminists. For *Seduction* actually *does* propose ways and means to erode the authority and power of 'the system', but it does so, using imagery that he must have realised would necessarily raise the hackles of women activists. The authoritarian (masculine) system has to be fought against, using the individual guile and wile of feminine seduction. Feminist strength, he avows, is its usage of unpredictability and uncertainty, whereby it wins over, only to subvert, the mighty male. All this but reinforces gender stereotypes and ultimately advises women to cajole or work behind the scenes, rather than stand up and demand their rights from an exploitative chauvinistic set-up. His feeble defence amounted to little; so what if, as he tells us, the feminine is 'ironic' in character and the 'masculine' is 'eccentric, paranoid and tiresome'? That is no improvement!

In conclusion, we cannot deny that, however off-putting his expressions may be, they pack a solid core of food for thought. The sign *does* often conceal an absence: witness the idealised masculinity or feminity that is concealed in the various advertisements that assail us on every side: they are simulation of a 'reality' that doesn't exist and yet people are trying to become precisely that. And when he declared that the Gulf War didn't take place, wasn't he but alluding to CNN's idealised projection on our television screens of 'smart bombs' homing onto their targets with no human loss or pilots' voices being heard describing what they're doing as if it were all an elaborate computer game being played before our eye. Still, if we discount, in all seriousness, any meaningful concept of the real – as he certainly does – isn't this tantamount to a feelingless and insensitive stance in the face of real human suffering? What would there be to prevent us from equally declaring that the Holocaust, the Babri-Masjid demolition and the consequent killings as well as the Staines' murders also 'didn't take place'?

Many of Baudrillard's remarks are reminiscent of Lyotard's broadsides against 'grand narratives'! But they lack the intellectual rigour and moral seriousness of the latter. For some he remains a guru of postmodernism, a 'sharp-shooting lone ranger of the pro-Marxist left' as one over-enthusiast has put it. But for most he is weak as a theorist: 'patience and immersion in the particular' are conspicuously absent in him, as Douglas Kellner puts it. Still, his studious cultivation of the provocative and the outrageous shouldn't deafen us to his often-insightful comments on the roles played by simulation and simulacra in constructing our vision of social reality.

7. Jacques Lacan (1901-1981)

Jacques Lacan was born on April 13, 1901, in Paris (he was to die there, too, on September 9, 1981). After graduating in medicine, he took up psychology and, after intensive research on paranoia, published his thesis on his patient, Aimée. He was to propose his 'mirror theory' of development, which won him a certain amount of fame and his views had some impact on radical thinkers like Saussure, Lévi-Strauss and Jacobson. He professed undying loyalty to Freud, which explains the fact that he was the only postmodernist to champion the notion of some kind of subject. His call for a 'back-to-the-basics' approach to Freudianism soon brought him into conflict with the rigidity and hard-line approach of orthodox disciples of the great guru, culminating in his expulsion from the International Psychiatric Association, IPA. Nothing daunted, he set up his own breakaway Ecole Freudienne in Paris in 1960 (the year after his excommunication), where he continued his famous 'seminars' until his untimely death.

The seminars were, in practice, something like extended lectures meant more or less exclusively for his awed disciples and his reputation came to be based upon these, later published as *Ecrits* (*Writings*). Peter Barry gives us a telling quote from one of the participants, which gives us an idea as to what it felt like to have sat in on them:

> He speaks in a wavering, syncopated or thundering voice, spiced with sighs and hesitations. He notes in advance what he is going to say, then, before the public, he improvises like an actor from the Royal Shakespeare Company… He fascinates his audience with his impressive language… Lacan does not analyse, he associates. Lacan does not lecture, he produces resonance. At each session of that collective treatment, the pupils have the impression that the master speaks about them and for them in a coded message, secretly destined for each one…[43]

For two to three hours a week, for almost a quarter of a century, Lacan would harangue his enthralled coterie of devoted auditors. The emphasis was clearly on showmanship, bypassing the more staid lecture format, so typical of French university life. He seemed to be consciously assuming the air of a prophetic figure, delivering an apocalyptic message to a select gathering of initiates. Maybe he had to do this to impress upon them that he alone had grasped the true teachings of Papa Freud.[44]

Already, before he got quite launched on his 'prophetic' phase, he had begun to promulgate views that would later set him on a collision course with conservative, dyed in-the-wool Freudians. Thus, in 1957, he gave an insightful lecture that is referred to nowadays as "The Insistence of the Letter". It was delivered not to a meeting of psychologists but to a 'lay' audience of students of philosophy (a 'lay' audience, in the sense that they were not trainee psychiatrists).

He began by posing a rhetorical question, "How could a psychologist of today not realise that his realm of truth is, in fact, the word?" He was not merely acknowledging the central place of language studies in the contemporary academic world. He was gradually building up his conviction that it is the workings of the unconscious self, rather than those of the 'conscious personality' (ego) that we should pay attention to. Indeed, breaking with the conventional teachings and approved doctrines of traditional Freudianism, he proposed the 'heretical' view that 'the kernel of our being' resides in the former, rather than the latter. And he would go one bold step further and maintain that the unconscious self functions in a far more logical and orderly (linguistic!) manner than had been thought in orthodox circles.

Freudian psychology, he emphasises, is essentially a verbal science and so fits perfectly well into the present-day set-up which awards to the linguistic sciences so crucial a place. "What psychoanalytic experience discovers in the unconscious is the whole fracture of language."

Now, if it *is* true that 'the unconscious is structured like a language', this would mean that it is structured as per the way contemporary linguistics holds that language is structured. This would imply, as we may recall, that meaning is a network of differences, i.e., contrasts between words and words, not between words and things. This but reinforces the watertight barrier, so to say, between the signifier (word) and the world of things (the referent). In other words, only the correlation between signifier and signified (reality, the 'referent' lies outside the system altogether) supply the standard for all research into meaning. No wonder, then, that "we are forced to accept the notion of an incessant sliding of the signified under the signifier".

As an example to illustrate 'slippage', let us take the word, or signifier, 'host'. Nowadays it has the connotation of friendliness, as when one talks of being welcomed by one's host. But it retains the older meaning of being an enemy, as is contained in the allied words, 'hostile': perhaps the link is understandable, for an unwelcome guest, or one who 'overstays his welcome' is resented and begins to be viewed as an enemy! Thus, meanings have an independent life of their own and may refuse to obey the alleged logical simplicities and rationalisation in which the 'external world' appears to incarnate.

All this is very well. But exactly where in Freud does Lacan think he is able to find a basis for his interpretation, thereby providing his defence against the charges of heresy by the IPA? His reply is that it is borne out by two 'dream work mechanisms' identified by the master, viz., 'condensation' and 'displacement'. The eminent-linguist and Lacanian scholar, Roman Jacobson, highlights their linguistic implications by renaming them, respectively, *metaphor* and *metonymy*, both forms of representation or 'making one stand for another'. In a metaphor, several things are compressed or condensed, as when we say, 'The ship ploughed through the water!' Here the movement of a ship through the water is compared to the work of a plough on the soil. Thus, in Freudian dream analysis, a person may dream of struggling to catch a train, running after it as it pulls out of the station and this is seen as a metaphor for his conviction that he's falling behind in some of his schedules or responsibilities and must make greater effort to 'catch up' on them. Metonymy is a figure of speech in which a part stands for the whole, For example, we may call out, 'All hands on deck!' – the 'hands' refer to the workers, a part (the hand) for the whole (worker). If one has a secret Latin lover, he/she may be represented in one's dream by an Italian car, a part (Italianness) for the whole (person).

Further confirmation for all this is found by Lacan in the fact that linguistic expressions are often used to manifest the articulations of the unconscious, as Freud himself observed: puns, allusions, slips of the tongue and the like. Thus, a person may, by a *lapsus linguae* whereby I refer to my brother, a seminarian, as one who has joined the 'cemetery' when I had intended to say, 'seminary'. According to Freud the word I use expresses my unvoiced, suppressed but unconscious feelings on the subject of my brother's vocation: he has said no to life and is living like a zombie, one of the living dead! This is clearly a break with the more prevalent western tradition, which, especially since Descartes, saw 'the kernel of our being' existing in the conscious ego, with one's unconscious playing, if at all, a secondary role. This is typified in Descartes' "I think, therefore I am!" It is the conscious, thinking I that constitutes me.

Lacan (who, it may be recalled, is addressing philosophy students) mischievously rephrases Descartes' dictum as, "I am where I think not!" In other words, it is the unconscious, rather than the conscious ego, which is my true self. The unconscious exists, as linguistic structure, before we enter into it: *that* is what is most basically me!

Finally, Lacan goes on to speculate how the conscious finally emerges. The most basic stage is that of 'the imaginary', where the child has no concept of its separate existence and has no notion of 'the other': it identifies itself with its mother. Then from about the age of six to eighteen months it undergoes 'the mirror stage'. Here, on seeing its image reflected in a mirror, the child gradually starts to form an idea of itself as a distinct being, unified and cut off from the rest of the world. Here is where the child enters into the language system, assimilating a sense of *lack* and *separation*, key Lacanian terms. These terms are crucial because language names what is not present (lack) and substitutes a linguistic sign for it (the signifier is 'separated' from the referent). This prepares the ground for the next stage, socialisation, which is marked with prohibitions and restraints, associated by Lacan with 'the father' and called by him 'the symbolic stage'. Feminists have seized upon this and pointed out that this is the world of patriarchal order and rationality arises. They speak of a nostalgia for the earlier, 'imaginary stage' which was beyond logic and grammar and, apparently, was more feminine. Both of these are necessary for our development and they must learn to co-exist though it should not unduly shock or scandalise us when, as in some postmodern literary works, one level irrupts into the other. In the novels of B S Johnson, for example, characters interact with the author and challenge his interpretation of the facts. We're back to the 'collapsing of boundaries' so beloved of postmodernists: the dividing line between author and his creation, between the person of the author and his fictitious characters merge into each other. Thus, we have 'meta fiction' or 'magic realism'!

8. Some Postmodernist Feminist Thinkers

Feminism burst upon the American (and continental, though a little later and not quite with the same intensity) cultural scene in the latter forties, in the aftermath of World War II. Since their men-folk had to be away at war, offices and factories had no choice but to recruit and train women to do what had been, until then, very much a male preserve. Soon there were women mechanics, engineers and dockyard workers (among others) and women proved themselves at least just as capable of men in doing all these 'men's jobs'. When the war ended, naturally, these women, who had proved themselves, refused to go back to their alleged 'women's world' of church, children and kitchens. They wanted their independent incomes and demanded their right to a career: why should only men be allowed access to certain jobs and cultural expressions when the war years had shown that women could do 'men's jobs' as well as and sometimes even better than their male counterparts?

Of course, demands for women's rights had surfaced long ago and, from time to time, in various cultures and at various moments in history, there had been sporadic protests and bold affirmations of feminism. Perhaps the first serious book, written by a woman on the subject, was Mary Wollstonecraft's, *A Vindication of the Rights of Woman* (1792),[45] just a few years after the French Revolution. Men had also written perceptively on that theme, from time to time, notably John Stuart Mill, in 1869 (*The Subjection of Woman*) and Friederich Engels, in 1884 (*The Origin of the Family*). Olive Schreiner seems to have 'jumped the gun' a bit, with her *Women and Labour* (1911), decades before the post-war feminist explosion. Virginia Woolf's *A Room of One's Own* (1929) would also fall into the same category. Simone de Beauvoir's epoch-making study, *The Second Sex* (1949) established the genre with, among other things, an interesting study of the portrayal of women in D H Lawrence.

Quite understandably, by the 1960s, feminism had become both vocal and stridently aggressive, with the 'burn-the-bra' brigade and other controversial movements. After a while, when the bottled-up bitterness and anger had been allowed sufficient abandon, more restraint and mellowness became manifest. Studies in feminist literary criticism proliferated and this was no reactionary wave: after all, as many feminist critics had pointed out, literature had played a major role in building up and buttressing the male chauvinistic society. It brainwashed us into accepting certain questionable 'role models' for the male and the female and indulged in explicit and implicit vitriolic comments against women who dared to aim at other things besides marriage and motherhood.

It is to Toril Moi and her insights on 'conditioning' and 'socialisation' that we are indebted for the now well-worn triple distinction between feminist, female and feminine: she defines these, respectively as, 'a political position' (the demand for women's share in the power usurped totally by men) 'a matter of biology' (the physiological fact of having certain sexual organs) and 'a set of culturally defined characteristics' (a construct, varying from culture to culture, but invariably determined by the dominant male ethos). Simone de Beauvoir is obviously using 'woman' in the last-named sense when she stages in the opening lines of her *The Second Sex*, "One is not born a woman, one becomes a woman."

Today, quite a number of feminist studies focus on the role of literature in the 'socialisation of woman'. It is an undeniable fact that literary works (especially novels) have played a great role in developing role models for men and women, in prescribing what is acceptable behaviour and what is not, for the male and the female. Thus, for instance, women in nineteenth century novels rarely do anything apart from housework and their happiness depends exclusively on what kind of men they can win over for themselves.

In the 1970s, the stress moves on to highlighting the 'mechanisms of patriarchy', the cultural mindset, whereby sexual inequality was perpetuated. Specific books and authors were singled out for attack and a combative, polemical tone becomes predominant. Thus Elaine Showalter summed up this decade from 'androtexts' (texts written by men) to 'gynotexts' (written by women). She introduces the concept of 'gynocriticism', the study of gynotexts. Its subject would include:

> the history, styles, themes, genres and structures of writing by women; the psychodynamics of female creativity; the trajectory of the individual or collective female career; and the evolution or laws of a female literary tradition.

The 1980s represent a period of 'mellowing down', as it were. In the first place, feminist writing became more open: it began to draw upon as wide a range of disciplines as Marxism, structuralism, linguistics, etc., to deepen its studies and analyses of the cultural situation of women. Secondly, it moved away from attacking male versions of the world to exploring the female worldview and reconstructing lost or suppressed records of female experience. Finally, it called for a writing of literary and religious texts from a woman's perspective.

Today, feminist studies proceed with considerable insight, along three important and not unrelated areas: feminism and literary theory, feminism and language and feminism and psychoanalysis. Let us explore each of these in some detail.

a. Feminism and Literary Theory

This, in itself, is a contentious issue among feminists. The English speaking ones (the Americans, more than the British) tend to be rather suspicious of using the insights of contemporary schools of philosophy in their studies. The Europeans, especially the French, make good use of post-structuralism and psychoanalytic theory in their research. Differing slightly from their American counterparts, the British tend to be socialist and Marxist in many of their approaches; French feminism, on the other hand, takes its cue from post-structuralists like Lacan, Foucault and Derrida. The major feminists today are all French nationals, viz., Julia Kristeva, Bulgarian born, who laments the fact that she is commonly taken to be the 'embodiment of French intellectualism', Hélène Cixous, Algerian born, and Luce Irigaray.

b. Feminism and Language Studies

This is the area which commands the most attention of feminists and there is a marked polarisation here, too: it focuses around the question as to whether there is such a thing as a language that is inherently feminine and whether language is non-neutral, whether language usage is gendered, due to the impress of male novelists who have been allowed to dominate the field, almost since its inception. Virginia Wool, in her *A Room of One's Own*, is quite convinced that there is and ruefully notes that, when a woman turns to write, she finds "no common sentence ready for her use": the established 'man's sentence' of carefully balanced and rhetorically patterned sequences was "unsuited for a woman's use", she declares. Some women novelists, notably Charlotte Brontë and George Eliot tried their hands at it, but failed.

Jane Austen, on the other hand (at least, in her judgment, i.e. Woolf's), 'devised a perfectly natural, shapely sentence for her own use', presumably less carefully balanced and patterned than male prose. Whatever, her thesis is that the would-be novelist who is a woman comes to her craft suffering from a severe handicap: she is labouring to employ what is, in effect, an exclusively male medium, made by males for masculine usage. Dale Spender, who wrote *Man Made Language* (1981) is in total agreement with her: language is not neutral but patriarchic and designed to further a patriarchal purpose.

There are, of course, feminists who beg to differ, for example, Sandra Gilbert and Susan Gubar. They totally decry all this talk of a 'feminist language' and a 'feminist style of writing' (*écriture féminine*, as Hélène Cixous puts it).

All three French feminists, Julia Kristeva, Hélène Cixous and Luce Irigaray are staunch supporters of *écritur féminine*. Hélène Cixous essays a halting descriptive definition of it, illustrating it with her own prose, replete with free play or meanings and a loose grammatical style:

> It is impossible to define a feminine practice of writing (*écriture féminine*), and this is an impossibility that will remain, for this practice can never be theorised, enclosed, coded... it will always surpass the discourse that regulates the phallocentric (i.e. male-dominated) system; it does and will take place in areas other than those subordinated to philosophico-theoretical domination. It will be conceived of by subjects who are breakers of automatisms, by peripheral figures than no authority can ever subjugate...[46]

This *écriture féminine*, it would appear, belongs to a realm beyond logic (it 'can never be theorised'...) and is used by a relentless warrior who battled unremittedly for liberation (involving 'peripheral figures' whom 'no authority can ever subjugate'). It is something unique to women and must be, not merely cultivated, but celebrated. She goes on:

> Women must write through their bodies, they must invent the impregnable language that will wreck partitions, classes and rhetorics, regulations and codes, they must submerge, cut through, get beyond the ultimate reserve-discourse, including the one that laughs at the very idea of pronouncing the word, 'silence'... Such is the strength of women that, sweeping away syntax, breaking the famous thread (just a tiny little thread they say) which acts for men as a surrogate umbilical cord.[47]

Now we have a few additional characteristics of *écriture féminine* to add to the preceding. It is boldly transgressive, knows no rules and hurries on its uninhibited way intoxicatedly, as it were. But Cixous is perhaps letting herself get carried away by her enthusiasm for it, for she ends up seeing the feminine body as immune ('impregnable') to social or gender conditioning ('rhetorics, regulations, codes') and able to maintain a kind of pure, unsullied feminine essence. But doesn't this contradict her avowed postmodernist conviction that there is no such thing as an objective feminine 'essence', which is not a social 'construct'? And isn't she advocating a kind of 'grand narrative', a kind of over-arching femininity, over and above all social and cultural differences – another anathema thesis for the postmodernists with whom she allies herself?

Julia Kristeva moved to Paris in 1966, bringing a uniquely East-European perspective to the fashionable structuralist atmosphere she found there. Roland Barthes says of her that she "subverts authority, the authority of monologic science", by destroying previous preconceptions, thereby helping her to shift from "a semiology of products to a semiotics of production."[48]

In her provocative essay, "The System and the Speaking Subject" she presented her now well known distinction between two aspects of language, the symbolic and the semiotic. The former maintained and popularised the illusory notion of a stable, unified self: it was 'a language with a foreclosed subject, or with a transcendental subject-ego'. A characteristically male language, it was associated with authority, order, 'the father', repression and control, that is to say, with 'the family, normalcy, normative classico-psychological-tending, all of which are just so many characteristics of fascist ideology.' Semiotic language, on the other hand, is more feminine, redolent with 'displacement, slippage, condensation'. It is less logical (if at all!) and prefers random connections and polysemy. It is the language of poetry and of conversation. Symbolic language is that of scientific research and exactitude, 'plain, unadorned writings', as the eighteenth century rationalists would say. Revealing a romantic streak, she likens it to Plato's *chora*, a kind of maternal language, a 'state of language anterior to the world'. Not all who use it are females: indeed, some of Kristeva's best exemplars of such semiotic language are male writers! But she is insistent that we ever remember that the symbolic and semiotic are not different *kinds* of language, but two different *aspects* of the same language and, what's more, they can occur in one and the same sample. She tries to strengthen her case by an appeal to the Lacanian notion of the conscious and the unconscious and sees this insight hinted at also in Saussure's 'network of differences'. Indeed, she avers, deconstruction can be seen as helping the unconscious to emerge from the text, to disrupt the conscious meaning. Various elements in post-structuralism seem to allude to this 'unconscious' or 'semiotic' dimension of language: gloating signifiers, random connections, improvisations, approximations, accidents, 'slippage' and a host of others. She then summons up Lacan's notion of the 'imaginary' and the 'symbolic phases' in human development to give yet further weight to her theory. The 'imaginary' is the pre-linguistic stage, where the child has not yet formed the notion of a distinct identity, separate from the rest of reality. She likens it to an idyllic, Eden-like state, free of all desire and any sense of deprivation, for how could the child feel any sense of 'lack', since he/she sees himself/herself as one with all there is? This 'feminine phase', Kristeva tells us, is 'politically subversive'. Then comes the 'symbolic' moment, when various conventions and norms of behaviour are foisted on the infant: it is taught its proper place, commanded to observe the rules of standard grammar and the cultural set-up: it is domesticated, controlled and made to conform to a given hierarchy – and all this is imposed on it according to a strict masculine, patriarchal model of doing and seeing things!

At this point, two possibilities are open to us, one more invidious and one more harmonious. The more dangerous approach is to continue the present trend, that of splitting everything into two neat watertight compartments, allotting the rational attitude to the world to men and the more emotive, intuitive and private area to women. Thus one would prolong the conflict and controversy between the sexes. A more balanced approach would be to recognise that both women and men need, from time to time, to take a rational way of viewing and handling things while, on other occasions, each should recognise that the alternative angle would be more relevant.

Luce Irigaray is, if anything, more radical than her feminist colleagues: she boldly challenges the patriarchal foundations of western metaphysics, as she calls them, and argues that women have been denied the status of subject within western culture. Lacan, Foucault, Derrida – all of these – she is convinced have, deliberately or not, worsened *la condition féminine*!

Psychoanalysis is governed by unconscious male fantasies; indeed, Freud's perspective is pronouncedly male and femininity is viewed in relation to the male model as a lack. Lacan's theory of the 'mirror stage' is an exclusively male account. Derrida deconstructs the masculine term in the male/female binary in such a way as to privilege the former (in spite of accommodating noises to the contrary). In the constructive part of her thought, Irigaray makes use of some interesting images, the most striking and well known of which are that of the 'two lips'. The two lips are neither one nor the other, but both: it is difficult to say where one identity begins and the other one ends. The contact of 'at least two lips' keeps woman in touch with herself, without any possibility of distinguishing what is touching from what is touched. This is very interesting, but it is not quite clear exactly what she is trying to say through this telling representation.

c. Feminism and Psychoanalysis

Irigiray's radical critique of Freudianism can serve as the transition to this final controversial area in the history of Semitist studies today. Indeed, feminism and psychoanalysis had a rather chequered relationship right from the start. Kate Millet's *Sexual Politics* (1969) roundly condemned Freud as the origin and source of just about every condemnable patriarchal notion current today. Apart from Irigiray, many other feminists share this conviction.

Juliet Mitchell, with her *Psychoanalysis and Feminism* (1974), sprang to the guru's defence and tried to show, drawing upon Millet's own vocabulary, that the master actually recognised the distinction between sex (a biological term) and gender (a construct). Freud did *not*, she argued, present the feminine as something 'given and natural' but a construct formed out of one's early experiences; hence it is malleable and changeable. Much of what he says should be read symbolically, not literally. Thus 'penis envy' should not be linked to the male sexual organ (whatever Freud might have meant by it), but as the feminine yearning to have access to power, which the male sex has appropriated to itself, with all its privileges. In the same way, Sandra Gilbert and Susan Gunbar, speaking of 'social castration', refer to women's lack of social power.

The rehabilitation of Freud is further sought by Jane Gallop, (*Feminism and Psychoanalysis,* 1982), by preferring to cite Lacan to Freud. In her opinion, the former makes more explicit what is only implicitly alluded to in the latter. The phallus, in Lacan, is definitely a symbol and does not point to the male sexual organ, as a perusal of Lacan assures us, she affirms and though men, avowedly, *do* come off better than women, in Lacan, yet they are also shown up to be also, to a certain extent, powerless too. Besides, Lacan's usage of puns, his playfully abstruse writings, his exploitation of 'paralogy' (going beyond logic) all seem to embody the feminine, semiotic aspect of language, rather than the masculine symbolic.

Generally speaking, however, French and British feminists seem more to rally to Freud's defence than their American counterparts. Witness Jerry Aline Flieger (one of the latter) writing with typical scorn on the Austrian psychiatrist's views

> I was fascinated and troubled by Lacan's characterisation of the phallus as the Signifier of Signifiers, as well as by his infamous statements, 'There is no sexual relation', and 'Woman does not exist'. Thus I was relieved and grateful when feminists such as Jacqueline Rose and Jane Gallop, in the late seventies and early eighties, performed ingenuous readings of Lacan as critics of phallocracy, rather than advocate…[49]

The strong note of incredulity and sarcasm in the above comment should be self-evident. But perhaps the reluctance of American feminists to accept the rehabilitation of Freud can be seen as stemming from the fact that psychoanalysis (having one's own personal 'shrink') is far more common in the US than on the continent.

Luce Irigaray, however, as we have seen, is one continental, who has no mercy for Freud. If Lacan was expelled from the IPA, her merciless and persistent attacks on Freud led to her expulsion from the Department of Psychoanalysis at Paris-Vincennes, headed by none other than the same Jacques Lacan. Still, it is a breath of fresh air to hear Jacqueline Rose asking us to listen to the voice of 'others', from cultures given no ear by either Freud or Lacan.

Feminism stresses the constructedness of femininity and emphasises the role of conditioning, socialisation and control played in this regard both by literature and by culture in general. But isn't all this tantamount to admitting some kind of 'given' essence of feminism – which flies in the face of the postmodern bias against 'essentialism'? And if one were to sincerely endorse 'anti-essentialism', wouldn't this make it difficult to make any generalisations about woman? And without some common perspective on woman, how could we have anything like 'feminism' at all?

Endnotes

1 Pannwitz, Rudolf, *Die Krisis der europaischen Kultur*. 1917 as cited by Mathew Illathuparampil in *Vidyajyoti*. Vol. 5, No. 8 (August 2001), p. 612.

2 Ibid.

3 de Onis y Sanchez, Federico, Antologfa de la poesae spaniola e hispano-americana (1881 - 1932). 1934. Illathuparampil, p. 612, footnote 25.

4 Illatuparampil, ibid.

5 Ibid., footnote 26.

6 Ibid. footnote 30.

7 Illathuparampil, p. 613.

8 de Saussure, Ferdinand, *Course in General Linguistics* (trsl. Wade Baskin), London, Fontana/Gollins, 1981 (Fourth Impression).

9 de Saussure, Ferdinand, *Course in General Linguistics* (trsl. Wade Baskin), London, Fontana/Gollins, 1981 (Fourth Impression), p. 120.

10 Ibid. p. 108.

11 Ricks, Christopher, "In Theory", in *London Review of Books*. April 1981, pp. 3-6. Quoted by Barry, Peter, *Beginning Theory*. Manchester, The University Press, 1995, p. 45.

12 Peter Barry, Op. cit.. p. 46.

13 Lévi-Strauss, Claude. *La Geste* D'Asdiwal. Paris, Imprimerie Nationale, 1958.

14 Ibid. p. 48.

15 Lévi-Strauss, Claude. *The View from Afar*. Chicago: University of Chicago Press, 1992.

16 Barthes, Roland, Riva Miller, and Ron Howard. *The Pleasure of the Text*. Oxford: Blackwell, 1990.

17 Powell, Jim, *Derrida for Beginners*. Hyderabad, Orient Longman, 2000, p. 9.

18 Quoted by Peter Barry, Op. Cit., p. 71.

19 Derrida, Jacques, *of Grammatology* (trsl. Gayatri Chakravorty Spivak), Delhi, Motilal Banarsidass Publishers, 1994.

20 Derrida, Jacques, *of Grammatology* (trsl. Gayatri Chakravorty Spivak), Delhi, Motilal Banarsidass Publishers, 1994, pp. 158, 163.

21 Johnson, Barbara, *The Critical Difference*. Johns Hopkins University Press, 1980.

22 Johnson, Barbara, *The Critical Difference*. Johns Hopkins University Press, 1980, p. 5.

23 It is this latter alternative which is the way we have viewed them in Cyril Desbruslais, *The Philosophy of Religion,* Jnana-Deepa Vidyapeeth, Pune (to be published).

24 *Of Grammatology*. p. 158.

25 Johnson, Barbara, *The Critical Difference*. Johns Hopkins University Press, 1980. p. 25.

26 Ibid., p. 163.

27 Ibid.

28 Ibid.

29 Op. cit.. p. 122.

30 Quoted by Hart, Kevin, "Jacques Derrida; The God Effect", in *Post-Secular Philosophy* (Phillip Blond, ed.), Routledge, London and New York, 1998, p. 261.

31 Lyotard, Jean-François. *The Postmodern Condition: A Report on Knowledge*. Minneapolis, Minn: Univ. of Minnesota Press, 2010.

32 Entry, "Jean-Francois Lyotard", in Sim, Stuart (ed.), *The A-Z Guide to Modem Literary and Cultural Theorists*. London, Prentice Hall, 1995, p. 271.

33 'Hysterectomy', remember, is an operation to cut out, or remove the womb.

34 The motto of Nazi Germany: affixed to the infamous Concentration Camp at Dachau.

35 Quoted by Fillingham, Lydia Alix, *Foucault for Beginners*. Hyderabad. Orient Longman, 2000, p. 67.

36 Quoted, Ibid., p. 85.

37 Ibid., p. 126.

38 Baudrillard, Jean. *America*. Milano: SE, 2009.

39 Baudrillard, Jean. *Cool Memories*. 1990.

40 Eugen Berthold Friedrich Brecht, known professionally as Bertolt Brecht, was a German theatre practitioner, playwright, and poet. Living in Munich during the Weimar Republic, he had his first successes with theatre plays, whose themes were often influenced by his Marxist thought.

41 Kellner, Douglas and Jean Baudrillard; *From Marxism to Postmodernism and Beyond*, Cambridge and Oxford, Polity and Blackwell, 1989.

42 Brooker, Peter (ed.), *Modernism/Postmodernism*. London, Longman, 1992, p. 154.

43 Quoted by Lechte, John, *Julia Kristeva*. London, Routledge, 1990, pp. 36-37.

44 Quoted by Peter Barry, op. cit. p. 123.

45 Wollstonecraft, Mary. *A Vindication of the Rights of Woman*, Aberdeen: Ockham Publishing, 2015.

46 Marks & de Courtivron, *New French Feminism*. New York, Harvester, 1981. Quoted in Peter Barry, op. cit.. p. 127.

47 Marks and de Courtivron, p. 256. Quoted by Peter Barry, p. 128.

48 Article, "Julia Kristeva", in Sim, Stuart (ed.), *The A-Z Guide to Modern Literary and Cultural Theorists*.

49 Flieger, Jerry Aline, *Changing Subjects; The Making of Feminist Literary Criticism*, quoted in Peter Barry, Op. cit.. p. 132.

PART THREE

POSTMODERNISM: A SCHOOL OR AN ATTITUDE?

Having studied the main views of some of the main postmodernist thinkers (and their precursors), we are in a better position to sum up the key themes that return, in various forms, throughout their writings. From here it might be a little easier to try and indicate what are the main ideas or causes that they uphold.

This is necessary, because there is a tendency nowadays to brand just about everything that is slightly unorthodox, not quite in keeping with traditional ways of doing things, as 'postmodern'. "Ours is a world that, for better or worse, has been labelled as postmodern", notes Paul Lakeland.[1] And, if we allow the term to be used as loosely as many of its enthusiasts do, reducing it to a kind of synonym for anything unconventional, we practically empty it of all depth and would perhaps miss the important insights and challenges it offers to our technocratic, consumeristic society and world.

As Madan Swarup, of South Bank University, London, points out, the term is at once universal and elusive:

> Postmodernism is being talked about and written about everywhere in contemporary Western society. The term postmodern is being used in many artistic, intellectual and academic fields. The figures associated with postmodernism include Rauschenberg, Baseliz, Schnabel, Kniefer, Warhol and, perhaps Bacon, in art; Jencksand Venturi in architecture; Artaud in drama; Barthes, Barthelme and Pychon in fiction; Lynch is film (Blue Velvet); Sherman in photography; Derrida, Lyotard and Baudriallard in philosophy. There are of course, other subjects that ought to be mentioned: anthropology, geography, sociology ... the list is endless and the names to be included lead to vigorous and bitter controversies. But just one thing is sure: postmodernism is of great interest to a wide order of people

> arid directs our attention to the change of a major order taking place in contemporary society and culture.[2]

Just what is this 'change of a major order' that is 'taking place in contemporary society and culture' that merits the qualification of 'postmodern'? Is it enough for something to be a departure from the traditional norm the called such? Would we be justified in labelling the shameful plight of the displacement of our adivasis, the pitiful treks of homeless refugees, the spate of terrorist attacks and hijackings as 'postmodern phenomena'? After all, they blur the timeworn and traditional geographic and political boundaries. And, when I improvise the Eucharistic prayer at Mass, laying aside the regulatory rubrics of the Roman Missal, am I celebrating a 'postmodern Mass'? Would we classify two popular Bollywood movies, of recent vintage, *Bombay Boys* and *Pyarmein Kabhi Kabhi* as 'postmodern films'? After all, in the former, the usual Hindi film cliché of the hero chasing the villain is contravened and, in the latter, we are given glimpses of the people behind the camera, breaking down the lines that divide the stars from the film-makers in the finished product? Or would my recent play, *Against the Tide*,[3] be a 'postmodern play' because, following the revolutionary approach of Brecht, 1 had characters speaking directly to the audience, breaking the dramatic tradition of a strict unbridgeable abyss between those who were on opposite sides of the proscenium?

I think that postmodern thought deserves more precision. After all, just about every school of philosophy considers itself as breaking with a past well-beaten path, boldly launching out on an untraveled trail. Would we call Kierkegaardian existentialism a 'postmodern' response to Hegelian idealism, or Ernst Bloch's critique of Marx a 'postmodern Marxism'? At that rate, all schools of philosophy would qualify to be called postmodern and the term would be emptied of all precise meaning.

Of course, I am not unaware that any attempt to try and cull from postmodern philosophical writings anything like a key 'doctrine' or a summary list of 'major postmodernist theses' would provoke a howl of protest from the postmodernists themselves. They would be quick to point out that it is not an 'ism', like idealism or rationalism – or even Catholicism – but a kind of attitude. John Deeley ventures to hail it as "a concept in search of a definition."[4] But even that remark would probably faulted by the postmodernists themselves, for it insinuates that postmodernism is something that could be enclosed within strict boundaries. Would it not be better to describe it as a movement? But, even here, we should proceed with caution for, as Max Charlesworth observes, "postmodernism is more a diffused mood than a movement, more a climate of thought than a philosophical system."[5] Indeed, as we have seen, many postmodernists prefer to speak of postmodernity, thereby avoiding the 'ism', which sounds too entrenched and static for their liking. However, if we end up saying that postmodernism is a mere 'attitude', it still remains too vague. In what consists this 'attitude' or 'mood'? As we have seen, it is no help to characterised it as mere 'avantgarde', a more or less revolutionary or radical approach to the norm. There are certain definite views that are inherent to postmodernism – or postmodernity (take your pick) and, the objections of postmodernists notwithstanding, I think it would be helpful for all of us, were we to clarify these. Else the timely warning of postmodernism would be lost behind a cackling chorus of real and pseudo-radical noises and slogans. Knowing that I am rushing in foolishly on to dangerous ground, I still venture to glean, from the thumb-nail sketches of postmodernists in the previous chapter, the more or less common themes and insights they have to offer.

1. Anti-Rationalism

Postmodernists, as a whole, seem to associate reason with domination, patriarchy, oppression, sterility and violence. However much they may or may not be at variance among themselves, this is one account on which they all seem to be in agreement. Incidentally, it would seem that reason has been the favourite whipping-boy of Western philosophy. In the Middle Ages, 'nominalism' berated it. In the Modem Period, empiricism attacked it and, in the first half of the twentieth century, it was existentialism that trained its big guns on it (postmodernism would take over the job in the second half!).

If modernism – at least, the Cartesian variety of it – had exalted reason, postmodernism would go against it. This was all sparked off by rationalism's penchant to trot out, at the drop of a hat, certain propositions as certain and universally binding truths, to be accepted by everyone, everywhere, or else ... As Foucault pointed out, most of these 'absolutes did not derive their pretentious claims from objective evidence or rational argument, as was commonly believed, but from the fact that they were being foisted on the hapless and helpless majority by a comparatively tiny but stronger and wealthier minority, who were using their might to bludgeon their 'truths' on to everyone else and thereby shore up their vested interests. The criterion of truth was, in effect, force and power. So George W. Bush would bomb, first Afghanistan' then Iraq, into submitting to his questionable concept of democracy and some high official would seek to oblige all Catholic priests, all over the world, to celebrate Mass according to his own private convictions. Rationalism, it seemed, could not but open the door to such flagrant abuse of power. And, to stem such abuses and cut away the ground from under the feet of reason's hob-nailed boots, did postmodernism profess its "incredulity to all grand narratives". On the other hand, it championed the right of each and every minority to assert its own 'little narrative'. This came as timely shot in the rare to many languishing oppressed action groups, who were trying to make their dissenting voices heard: dalits, adivasis, women, gays, etc.

2. Anti-Subjectivism

All the above excesses had been linked to the modernistic subject, as spawned by the founding father of rationalism, René Descartes. It was the disembodied, isolated and individualistic Cartesian ego which arrogated to itself the exclusive right to decide what was true and certain, and thereby fabricate grand narratives, to be ruthlessly imposed upon the 'recalcitrant and ungrateful ignorant masses'. This kind of questionable and over-weaning 'subject', which claimed intellectual domination over all objects and epistemological suzerainty over all 'lesser' subjects, was all too rightly called into question by critical postmodernists. And the flimsy edifice crumbled, like a pack of cards, under the onslaught ... and with it went the whole proud structure of naïve subject-centred philosophy. It was shown up for what it was: a mere construct. It was not merely 'influenced' by a diversity of external factors; it was constructed, lock, stock and barrel, by them. Only one postmodernist of repute would uphold some kind of subject – Lacan. That is partly because of his Hegelian roots and mainly because of his professional identity as a psychologist.

3. Anti-Humanism

With the death knell of the self or subject, "that spoilt brat of (modern!) philosophy,"[6] the end of the human person was announced. As the more sensationalist among the postmoderns never tired of repeating, "Nietzsche's 'God is dead' is old hat. We proclaim the death of main", was referring to the modernist attempt to place man (the gender bias is part of the idea) at the centre of all sciences and disciplines every-thing was valued and honoured solely in terms of its relevance to man, which, in concrete, meant it terms of what advantages it had to offer to the white, male Christian – preferably of the European variety. Now this postmodern salvo was a deliberate and rude blow to Sartrean humanism. Whence emerged a totally de-centred world. There was no longer a fixed and stable centre for things to revolve around – neither in man nor anywhere else. This is borne out by Derrida's "metaphysics of absence": there is no solid 'presence', no 'transcendental signified', around which everything could turn in orderly fashion and which would assign to everything else its place and price in some grand scheme of things.

4. Some Other Implications

Some other implications of postmodernism may be summed as follows:

a. The Primacy of the Surreal

In effect, there is no subject (it is a mere 'construct') and we cannot attain any objective and universal knowledge about real. No wonder, then, that the all-powerful media (in the hands of those who hold money and wield power) should offer us a pseudo-reality that would eclipse the actual world about us. Far from mirroring, or faithfully depicting, reality, the television screen and the front pages of our newspapers, create it: the media are not just King, they are God, the Creator. Baudrillard's "the Gulf war did not take place" is a provocative way of telling us that the only 'Gulf War that we ever knew was the sanitised, censored version of it that CNN and the other powerful new magnates allowed us to see. The real, cruel, ugly reality of that horrendous conflict was hidden from us - deliberately. And the "American way life", so hallowed and celebrated by the media a fiction only realised in Disneyland - certainly not in the ghettoes of Harlem, any more than in the jaded opulence of Beverley Hills.

But, don't we find this 'hyperrealism' (the fact of the imaginary world being given more credibility and attention than the real one) in our India today? Thus, the underprivileged masses, from time to time, take a break from the painful world of their daily life, to escape into the celluloid world of Bollywood, with its posh houses and lavish lifestyles, where justice and love always triumph – with a little bit of help from the current matinee idols. The more sophisticated among us devote hours to religiously follow interminable 'soaps' like *The Bold and The Beautiful*, rearranging our social and private life around the call of the idiot box. Hasn't TV become the new 'opium of the people'? Isn't there a clear blurring of the border between the real and the imaginary — and isn't this what the postmodernists are denouncing when they decry the hyperreal ruling our lives?

b. Epistemological Non-certainty

In medieval times was believed that theology (divine revelation) — and, to some extent, philosophy – was the sole and authentic dispenser of universal truth and certitude All this ended with the Enlightenment, most of whose adepts rejected religious faith as one with naïve superstition and naught else. Soon dawned modernism, where science – at last! – came into its own. Now science became the new religion. the men of science constituted its priesthood and findings were the sole dogmas that could our unwavering assent, then came Heisenberg, relativity and the quantum theory (to mention a few) and science's pretensions took quite a bashing. Everything was "merely an interpretation! one way of looking at things among many. The modernistic Cartesian/Lockean/Kantian subject, whose pure disembodied and objective gaze could sweep the whole outside world under its 'cognising' ken and could pronounce on its ontological status, wag effectively exposed for the fraud and illusion it was. Everything was slipping into the limbo of *sous erasure*, alas, for historical reasons we were stuck with these detached signifiers, compelled to employ them in communication *as if* they were pointing to real things 'out there', whereas, in fact, they were doing no such thing. Nothing is objective.

Nothing is certain. It's all a matter of words pointing to other words e words whose 'meaning' depends solely on how they happen to be situated in a syntagmatic chain. with reference to other words. Every view, any view, is as good as any other. There is no criterion of truth (apart from the brute force wielded by those currently in power). For Practical purposes, we would be advised to fall back on pragmatic guide. lines: if a particular 'truth' or belief 'works', 'for you, affirm it, as long as it does, That's all!

c. Morality at the Crossroads

This is the inevitable result of throwing out all metanarratives along with all universal truths. If all absolutes are rejected, there can be no criterion of truth, nor of morality. For all such criteria would be by definition, transcultural and transhistorical, valid at all times, in all places and for all people short, metanarratives. At most, one might tolerate a kind of mini - narrative, a somewhat limited criterion of truth or morality, valid on - for a restricted cultural or ethnic sub-group (but even here one could raise the question as to how it could have such limited universal applicability).

d. A Disenchanted Universe

Postmodernism has profound implications for religion in general and for theology in particular. Apart from ruling out the existence of any reality that could be called 'God' (the transcendental signified), the role of any believing community (such as the Catholic or Protestant churches) in a postmodern world, traditional dogmas, such as the uniqueness of Jesus and his universal salvific role are also called into question.

Further, many recent developments in contemporary science seem to lend credibility to the relativistic agnosticism that seems to characterize the spirit of postmodernism. Naïve scientism as well as logical positivism had to give way to the uncertainty principle quantum mechanics and chaos theory (to name but a few). If certainty and objectivity were all that we were faced with, as some postmodernists argue, this would not render the universe really mysterious and enchanting. It would merely become one that we could never know exhaustively. Postmodernism, however, tells us that we cannot know the world at all, in any meaningful serosa of the, term. A relativistic world is not mysterious or enchanting: it is plain disconcerting. That's all!

Endnotes

1 Lakeland, Paul, *Postmodemity: Christian Identity in a Fragmented World*, Nashville, Abingdon Press, 185, ix.

2 Sarup, Madan, *An Introductory Guide to Post-Structuralism and Postmodernism.* Athens, Georgia, The University of Georgia Press, 1993, p. 123.

3 Cyril Desbruslais is famous for his annual plays with social and revolutionary themes which he has been regularly scripting and acting for more than 35 years. Here Desbruslais is referring to one of them. [Editor's note]

4 "Quid sit Postmodernismus?", in Ciapolo, Roman T. (ed), *Postmodernism and Christian Philosophy*, New York, Random House, 1991, p. 79.

5 In 'Postmodernism and Theology", Ciapolo (ed.). op. clt., p. 188.

6 The phrase is from Lévy-Strauss.

PART FOUR

SOME CRITICAL COMMENTS ON POSTMODERNISM

Ever since Aristotle gave us that nifty definition of the human person, "Man is a rational animal" (yes, the Stagyrite did use sexist language), this has been the most succinct definition of our species. This was further encouraged by Aquinas' championing of the same: after all, it is an excellent definition, as definitions go, *per genus proximum et differentia specifica*.[1] It singles us out from the lesser denizens on the evolutionary chain: our capacity to reason – our distinctive ability to transcend the boundaries of the senses, of the here and now ... so as to attain the metaphysical, the transnatural, even God. Indeed, the Age of Reason, the Enlightenment, hailed reason as the Great Emancipator. It would liberate us from the obscurantism, ignorance and superstition of the 'Dark' or 'Middle' Ages, when an alleged reactionary Church, with-its ever-watchful Hounds of the Lord, would seek to suppress all independent and critical thinking with excommunications and burnings at the stake. Rationalism was supposed to usher in a Brave New World and lead humans ever valiantly on along sure paths of freedom, justice and happiness to the promised land of Peace and Prosperity.

But today, in the attack on reason, spear-headed by postmodernism, we and our contemporaries tend to look down at reason. Reason and rationality are bad words for us; many of us feel insulted to be dubbed 'rationalists'. Nowadays, reason is looked upon as the Father and Origin of all Ills: domination, patriarchism, violence, sterility and worse. What went wrong? Why this radical shift of allegiance?

1. René Descartes (1596-1650): The Villain of the Piece

As far as I am concerned, it is the Cartesian variety of rationalism that had given reason its bad name. The questionable understanding of rationality devised by

Descartes and his followers was further accepted and popularized by some of his most prominent adversaries (Locke, Kant and others of their ilk). And when postmodernists rightly attacked this spurious form of rationalism, they made the colossal blunder of thinking that the caricature they were debunking was the genuine article.

However, as Jürgen Habermas hastens to remind us, only a rehabilitated and authentic rationality can save us from the very real dangers that Descartes and co. are hurrying us towards. Postmodernism tried to rescue us from that by rejecting reason and rationality but this proved to be, if anything, a noble failure. For in spite of its avowed protestations of championing the cause of neglected and overwhelmed minorities, it ended up immobilizing both them and their would-be liberators in a quagmire of relativism and skepticism. Not only does this bequeath us even greater pitfalls than it is trying to help us avoid, it renders meaningless any possible in-depth communication between struggling humans (we can't even tell each other if we're in the same boat).

In the same way, it was only the bogus Cartesian subject, disembodied, isolating and hovering in solitary splendour above the things of this world that was effectively shot down by the penetrating criticism of Foucault et al. It was the ego of Descartes' philosophy that postmodernism interred once and for all – and good riddance! This 'spoilt brat' is not the authentic subject that Ken Wilber and those of his ilk (me, for instance) celebrate. That, in a nutshell, is my own critique of postmodernism. But let's get down to this in more detail.

a. A General Comment on Cartesian Rationalism

When we chorus that we are 'rational animals', we should not take this to mean that each and every one of our decisions – consciously or unconsciously – is hammered out on the anvil of pure reason alone. It's not as if, whenever we are confronted with a difficult choice, we have a kind of interior intellectual discernment to establish what would be the most logical, moral and rational way to act and then simply go ahead and do it, as if what we call 'freedom' were a mere act of reason, clothed in some more or less emotional garb. This is the impression that most rationalists – notably Leibnitz – convey. Actually, rationalists are always somewhat embarrassed and discomfited by the phenomenon of human freedom: it upsets their nice little apple-cart of orderly and predictable human behaviour. Unpredictability is not welcome in a rationalist *Weltanschauung*, despite various polite noises made in favour of indeterminism.

At this juncture, let us take a closer look at the views of Gottfried Wilhelm Leibnitz (1646 – 1716), Descartes' dedicated disciple, whose views, in my opinion, are quite typical in the whole issue of human decision-making. In his *On the Art of Combination*,[2] as also in his better known treatise *Monadology*,[3] he expressed his conviction that all logical predicates – be they truth of reason or truths of facts – are pre-contained in their subjects. In other words, even the free decisions of human beings could be rationally 'deduced' with infallible and predictable accuracy if only we were vouchsafed a glimpse into their complex personalities in too. Unfortunately – at present, at least – only God has such knowledge. One could contrast this simplistic view with the Scholastic notion of God's *scientia media* (middle knowledge) of free human choices and 'pure possibles'. One gets the impression that the rationalist Leibnitz was quite convinced that, given a bit more scientific advancement, such convenient deduction and predictability would fall within the purview of human knowledge as well. Freedom is swallowed up in rationality.

However, human decision resides precisely in the fact that, we – even after a long and laborious process of rational reflection and discernment – are not compelled from within, in any way, to follow the counsel of our intellect or conscience, which represents to us the most rational or moral thing to do. We can – and experience bears out that often we do – fly in the face of reason and conscience and choose precisely what is irrational and immoral. It is that which constitutes human freedom – which is the act of a faculty other than the intellect and it is by no means obliged to follow the behests of the latter.

b. A General Comment on the Cartesian Subject

The Cartesian human subject, that questionable legacy of Descartes to modem philosophy, is founded on a very serious oversight – one that strongly undermines its Validity, even its very identity. While elaborating his famous '*cogito-ergo-sum*' starting point, consciously or no, Descartes had taken inspiration from St Augustine (the founding-father of rationalism never ever, acknowledged his indebtedness to previous thinkers; on the contrary, he naïvely persisted in his conviction that he was restarting 'everything from scratch'). Against the skeptic claim that we humans cannot know anything for sure, the Saintly Bishop of Hippo had retorted, "Si fallor, sum!" (in other words, even if I am in error, 1 can still be sure of, at least, my existence!). In other words, no matter what else I doubt, no matter what collection of erroneous views I mistakenly hold as true, of one thing I can be absolutely sure: my existence. For how could I be in error if I were not to exist? And if I can thus show I can attain at least one item of sure and certain knowledge, this is tantamount to a refutation of the central thesis of skepticism, that we are not able to attain any truth. Thence, we may proceed to establish certain other truths, equally sure, that are also implied in that pristine affirmation. Hence, can we explicate the conditions under which we can arrive at certainty in knowledge.

Now, it is quite legitimate to refute skepticism by a straightaway appeal to some element of my intellectual knowledge (the awareness of my own existence as being inseparably linked to my awareness of being in error or in the state of doubt). One can do this, quite legitimately, by bypassing sense knowledge and one's own embodiedness (at least explicitly). But if I pass, thence, to the establishment of the nature and structure of the ego (as Descartes did), we're on extremely shaky ground.

For 'I think' cannot be taken as the starting point for human philosophising, for the simple fact that we humans don't – can't – initiate any human activity by doing it in the abstract. We don't 'just think' we always think something concrete, be it "shoes and ships and sealing-wax" or "cabbages and kings". I cannot say, 'Cogito' (I think) before I have said '*Cogito aliquid*!' (I think something). Nor is even this latter an authentic starting-point, because thinking always presupposes some sense- experience as having gone before it. As the old scholastic axiom goes, "*nihil in intellectu nisi per prius in sensu*" [There is nothing in the human intellect that hasn't been first in the senses!] The launching pad of human thought is sense experiences there is no short cut to thinking without this preliminary step. Of course, human thinking is not limited to what can be sensibly experienced. We are able to transcend matter, the boundaries of space and time, to literally go 'out of this world.' As Rahner so succinctly put it, we are spirits (i.e. capable of transcending this world of material things) only because we are rooted in this world of matter. For us no world means no transcendence. Therefore, Descartes' starting-point should have been *sentio aliquid* [I sense something concrete]. Had he recognized this then he would have been able to note that humans are not capable of pure sensation or pure intellection (the two activities inter-penetrate, actually). Then would he have also recognized that my body is as much part of my make-up, as my soul. The "spoilt brat of philosophy" (the phrase is from Levy-Strauss) is Descartes' disembodied, individualistic ego, a caricature of the human subject. "I, that is, my soul..." Descartes would write, effectively reducing the human person to a kind of ethereal incorporeal substance.

I am *not* a thinking thing *pace* Descartes:[4] I am an embodied, concretely existing sensing thing and, only later, a thinking being. 1 am not so much 'a spirit incarnate in my body', as the traditional phraseology tends to put it. Rather am I "a spirit incarnate in the world through my body". The essence of the human condition is, to borrow an expression from the French existentialist Gabriel Marcel, (he'd rather describe himself as "a Christian Socratist"), "to be in a situation". One cannot give even a "pointer definition" of the human person, one cannot come anywhere near to grasp what it means to be human, if ones leave out human essential rootedness-in-the-world. Doing that would be like taking a fish out of water, in order to study it. We are spirits in the world; a spirit out of the world might define an angel, not a human being. And, once again, let it be remembered, that we are not using 'spirit' in the traditional; sense of the antithesis of matter, but in the Rahnerian meaning of that which is capable of transcending.

Far from being that disembodied, isolated individual that Descartes represented it to be, the human subject is an incarnate spirit, necessarily rooted in this world and thereby inextricably bound in communion and dialogue with other spirits as also 'the things of this world'. It is only in, and through a continuous and continual mutual interchange with all of these, that we can attain any truth or certainty - about ourselves, as much as about the world we live in. And, in the vast majority of cases, we never arrive 'once and for all' at any absolute and universal truth. Experience and research, more often than not, yields us ever newer and more insightful discoveries and perspectives. Truth, most times, is something that we approach as an ever receding horizon. And truth/ being is something we must ever seek in all we do – hot as a choice, a hobby or a fad, but as a-bounded duty. This is what Heidegger meant when he described the human person (Dasein, or more accurately, daSein) as "the Shepherd, or Caretaker, of Being": if we don't take our responsibility to Being (and *b*eing*s*, I may add) seriously, there is no one else in the world who can!

The postmodernists rightly rail against the Cartesian ego subject, the bane of modem philosophy. And when this latter has the effrontery and gall to arrogate to itself the absolute prerogative to bath sole arbiter of what is true and real and what is not, the attack on it becomes all the more justified. But this is only a pseudo-ego, not the genuine article. Postmodernists don't seem to realise that in their continued rejection of the Cartesian ego as the authentic subject, they are like Don Quixote tilting at windmills. They ate taking potshots at a scarecrow, a man of straw. The real thing is made of sterner stuff. It is located securely within this world, beings and Being encompass it (Jasper's *das Umgreifende*) and, as we have seen, it is no isolated entity: it is ever engaged in an active and attentive dialogue with all else and it is only thereby that it realizes its goal of a better understanding of all that is.

2. Blaise Pascal (1623-1662): Absolute Rationalism is Irrational

Absolute rationalism is espoused by those who hold that naught but pure reason would be our guiding principle throughout life. "No superstitions, no blind faith, no dogmatisms," such people would naïvely expostulate, "We'll only accept what can be established within the demanding courts of reason alone!" Such a stance is typical of all who have been bitten by the bug of Cartesian/modernistic rationalism. And, if at first sight, such a position sounds very sane and reasonable, as the only philosophical approach worthy of a full-blooded *animal rationale*, perhaps second thoughts might lead us to review this hasty opinion as the immature, irresponsible and anti-human posture it is. But let's not anticipate.

It was Blaise Pascal (1623-1662) who, in spite of having basked somewhat in the sun of Descartes' thought, penned those oft-quoted lines in his *Pensées*. "The heart has its reasons which the reason cannot know." And how right he was! Some of our most basic, soul-searching and far–reaching choices are the fruit of the sobering assessments of reasonable risk, not pure reason alone. Interpersonal convictions – such as, the grounds on, which we trust our friends, choose our life's partner and decide what is our 'vocation' in life – none of these are, or can be, made on the basis of rational argumentation. They do not partake of the class of mathematical and scientific certitudes – 'truths' of which we cannot reasonably harbour even a shadow of doubt. But this does not mean that such commitments are come by on whimsy or caprice – something like, for instance, a child's belief in fairies. This has no foundation in reality, no reasonable basis on which to take ones stand. A mature person can point to *some* clear evidence in favour of such personal stances one doesn't blindly 'plump for them' for no rhyme or reason. But the evidence, significant though it may be, is not sufficient to give cogent and compelling motives in its favour; it can't remove all possible doubt. Nor is such a personal conviction the result of impetuosity, unbridled haste and childish lack of self-control. It is *impossible in principle* to ground these options on the bulwark of solid and unadulterated reason.

Reason plays an important and indispensable role in many spheres of life, but it has its limitations and it would be irrational to demand more of it. Our nature as rational animals is often expressed more through actions stemming from reasonable risk than proceeding from ratiocination, pure and simple.

It would even' be irrational – or impractical, to be more precise – to press for absolute rationalism in even those areas where rationalism *can* work. Were, one to demand strict adherence to the code of rationalism in such cases, it would render human life effectively impossible. One would not be able to take a meal in a decent restaurant (or even in one's family!) without lugging along a whole laboratory to analyze the food and drink that one was planning to consume (maybe it had been – even inadvertently – poisoned?).

Nor would one be able to climb into a bus or any form of public transport before demanding that everyone – including the driver and conductor – submit to a strict security check (one of them could be an escaped homicidal maniac or a terrorist! Nor could one even venture to breathe in surrounding air before scientific analysis could ensure that there were no toxic substances in it ... and so on. At every turn and twist of life, we are forced to take reasonable risks – and we do so, without batting an eye-lid. It's reasonable to suppose – and unreasonable to doubt – that the food we eat at home or in a restaurant will not be poisoned, that my fellow passengers in a bus are as normal and harmless as I and the air I breathe is as healthy as one can reasonably expect polluted urban air to be. Insisting on costly and time-consuming checks and security tests would probably end up making oneself friendless ... and firmly ensconced in the psychotic ward of a mental hospital. Absolute rationalism is dangerous for one's psychic health.

3. Jürgen Habermas (1929-): Rehabilitator of Reason

One of the most celebrated thinkers of the Frankfurt School of Critical Philosophy, Habermas is well aware of the strengths of reason and its weaknesses. Born at Dusseldorf in 1929, he spearheads the contemporary European response to the excesses of postmodernism, especially its debunking of its version of modernistic 'subject-centred philosophy', together with its enthronement of reason. He is of the opinion that postmodern thinkers (especially Nietzsche and his two major disciples, Heidegger and Derrida, arguably the most respected gurus of the movement) were unable to skirt the very pitfalls they had decried in the Cartesian legacy. He called for a rehabilitation of authentic rationality which, according to him, was the only way to steer a safe path between the Scylla of oppressive Cartesian rationalism and the Charybdis of postmodemistic bewildering relativism.!

In the first place, all the noble liberative pretensions of the postmodemistic resolve turn to dust and ashes. They had begun with a praiseworthy purpose: to silence the commands of the rich and powerful, who were foisting – by sheer brute force, propped up by the almighty dollar/euro/pound sterling – their private, vested-interest-ridden 'truths' as absolutes on the hapless and helpless masses of the Third World. They had showed up the hypocrisy and injustice masquerading behind all the discourse of criteria of truth and foreign aid. But, in the heat of the battle, they had shot themselves in their own feet, immobilizing their own warriors only a few minutes after the battle had begun! For, in the relativistic, 'anything goes' kind of epistemology they implicitly support, they cannot give us any good reason as to why the oppressed masses/minorities should revolt at all! If one view is as good as any other, what grounds have these latter to reject the oppressor's value system and *Weltanschauung* in favour of their own – if not seek to impose their own on him *en revanche* (which is what revolutions are all, about)? For they cannot speak of anything like "natural rights" or of duties and responsibilities inherent to "human dignity", as they would be tantamount to trotting in through the back door the metanarrative of human nature that they had unceremoniously ushered out through the front! One could not bravely go to the rescue of a woman about to be raped or even summon the police if he were drunken next-door neighbour beat up his hapless wife and helpless children: that would imply a value-judgment on the miscreant's behaviour, derived from one's personal "narrative" being absolutised. Nor could dalits, oppressed women, bonded labourers, sexually abused children and displaced indigenous people band together to find unity in their strength: as per the postmodernistic doctrine that there is no basic human nature (indeed, no real subject at all) they'd have nothing on which to ground an alleged common identity. The initially laudable intervention of the postmodernists to liberate the downtrodden from their oppressors leaves them no better off than before. They end up isolated individuals who do not – worse, cannot – come together on any shared basis to chalk out, and fight to realise, any common vision or goal. They're back at the tender mercies of their oppressors.[5]

But, then – as Habermas, so pointedly asks – what else can we expect? If, with Heidegger and Derrida, we fulminate against the "decadence of reason" and ridicule all that transcends space and time (metaphysics, theology and morality), what else remains to function as the (pseudo-) criterion of truth but power, brute physical force, allied to international market forces (a terrible "absolute" if ever there was one)? Nietzsche's "Will to Power" is given free rein and it will be the norm of truth, morality and culture and there's nothing to challenge it. Modernism had enthroned reason (or rather, a caricature of it). Postmodernism would dethrone this caricature (taking it for 'the real thing') and enthrone "artistic taste" in its place. And isn't this an "absolutisation of "*de gustibus non est disputandum*? or, in everyday language: "One must not dispute about tastes": I like coffee and you like tea and it's pointless arguing about who's right!

But Habermas hasn't finished yet. In the first place, as he penetratingly asks, how can 'taste', be made *the* organ of knowledge without,' in some way, re-instating the subject-centred philosophy that the postmodernist has been so loudly rejecting? Is not the true basis of judgment, not taste, but argumentation? And isn't argumentation founded on logic, not taste? Power, after all, is but a variation of taste and aesthetics and has nothing to do with logic. Thus, substituting "taste" for logic saves us neither from power-domination nor from subject centred ism. Only authentic rationality, re-instated, can.

Derrida, for his part (Habermas notes), sought to overcome the centrality of reason and its absolutising penchant by exalting the supremacy of aesthetics over logic. But this meant having to steamroll all literature into one single genre, that of aesthetics, and philosophy and science hardly qualify to make that grade. Thus, in effect, he confused three types of validity claims: the correct (operative more in the realm of aesthetics), the truthful (epistemology) and the liberative or emancipatory (ethics or morality). Nor does he distinguish between how equally different types of speech acts. There is, first the more specialized type of exchange which is concerned with problem-solving: the issue of truth is very relevant here. On the other hand, there is a wide disparity of other kinds of human interaction that are not at all so engaged: conversational transactions that could be serious or non-serious, fictive, parodic or jocose and so on. They have nothing in common with theorizing, proving and such, which characterize the first type. The significant point is that Derrida, like Heidegger before him, has neither been able to disentangle himself from a philosophy of the subject nor has he been able to shrug off reason![6]

In conclusion, Habermas points out that postmodern thinkers do a good job as regards the negative part of their philosophy. They bring out very well the Cartesian error of an all powerful, self-referential subject, acting in solitary spiritual isolation and objectifying all that comes under its purview. But they were unable to propose a worthwhile alternative to correct that wrong approach. Their presuppositions remained tied to the very subject-centred philosophy they were laboring to repudiate.

> Only a reason to which we ascribe a 'power of the keys' could either include or exclude. Hence, inside or outside are linked with domination and subjugation; and the overcoming of reason-as-power-holder is linked with opening the prison gates and vouchsafing release into an indeterminate freedom. Thus the other of reason remains the mirror image of reason in power.[7]

In other words, what we need is a new paradigm, incorporating the positive insights of postmodernism, correcting the errors of medernism and this involves not a rejection of reason but a re-discovery of authentic reason. This involves seeing knowledge as a process of understanding in an inter-subjective mode, characterised by mutual agreement and understanding communication, which, in turn, would call for an inter-subjective reason, reestablishing broken relationships through communication, avoiding subject-centred objectivism.

4. Ken Wilber (1949-): Rehabilitator of the Subject

The first philosopher-psychologist to have his Collected works (eight volumes) published in his own life-time,[8] Ken Wilber was born in Oklahoma (USA), in 1949. After trying his best to study and learn through various Universities and after various false starts in various disciplines, he decided to educate himself by following his own curriculum, travelling widely and trying to integrate his insights culled from disparate readings in psychology, medicine, science, literature and religion – East and West. His *The Spectrum of Consciousness* (1976),[9] published when he was only 27, won for him a reputation as an original thinker with excellent, penetrating and integrative insights into psychology and culture, oriental and occidental.

	Internal	**External**
Individual	Consciousness Worldviews Values Purpose Knowledge	Behavior Habits Skills Communication
	Culture	**Systems**
Collective	Shared Values Shared Purpose Social Norms History	Structure Processes Agreements Metrics

His key insight of the "Four Quadrants"[10] is of great relevance here: it not only offers us a more contemporary and rewarding vision of the human subject, but also provides us the basic framework for his interesting and original comments on premodernism, modernism and postmodernism. He had studied and compared the developmental maps of various thinkers – ways of studying the process of biological, psychological, cognitive and spiritual development of individuals. It gradually dawned on him that the development of any individual could be seen in four quadrants described above.

System Sciences

Just as the lower left is the plural or collective-aspect of the upper left (and both cover the subjective or interior dimension of consciousness), i.e. from I to WE, so the upper right is the plural or collective aspect of the upper, right (and both these express the exterior or behavioral dimensions, correlates of their corresponding subjective or interior sides), i.e. from IT (singular) to ITS (plural). Thus the upper right focuses on phenomenological observation of individual organisms and the precise recording of that data. On the other hand, the lower right studies (also at a detached, third person level) such data obtained from collections organisms.

This is the level of the "system" sciences (as opposed to the "individualistic" sciences), such as sociology, anthropology, political set-ups and so on. Thus we can combine both these- quadrants into one (*Science*: the level of Its) and end up with a 'Big Three' of the Quadrants: 1 (*Aesthetics*), We (*Morals*) and Its (*Science*). This is important for any integral project must embrace all three dimensions or it'll end up truncated!

	Subjective/Interior	**Objective/Exterior**	
Individual	*Upper Left* **I-ART** *INTENTIONAL*	*Upper Right* **IT – SCIENCE** *BEHAVIOURAL*	Individual
Collective	*CULTURAL* **WE-MORALS** *Lower Left*	*SOCIAL* **ITS-SCIENCES** *Lower Right*	Collective
	Subjective/Interior	Objective/Exterior	

Upper Left: Intentional Sphere of individuals; subjective consciousness; bodily sensation; mental ideas, soul, spirit, Aesthetics or ART

Upper Right: Behavioral/objective correlate of consciousness (upper left); language of 3rd person; objective accounts of individual sciences, facts or SCIECNCE.

Lower Left: Cultural sphere, i.e., collective reflections of individuals in a group, we/I-thou language. MORALS

Lower Right: Social, objective, exterior forms (institutional), expressions of lower left, production systems. SYSTEM SCIENCES.

Now, this is precisely what happens under postmodernism (as in modernism and premodernism, too, as we shall see): it is a *Weltanschauung* which gives pride of place, if not exclusivity, to one single quadrant over all the others and the result is a lop-sided, biased view of reality. It is at this stage that Wilber brings in the insight of holarchy, a very helpful term that he has borrowed from Koestler. It refers to what could be called a 'natural hierarchy', which is characterised by inclusiveness, ever increasing wholeness, best exemplified by letters of the alphabet that combine to form words, which – in their turn – come together to form sentences ... thence to paragraphs, sentences, chapters and so on. Holarchy needs to be demarcated clearly from an associate term, hierarchy, which is built on control and exclusivity. In this sense, we can speak of the "Great Holarchy of Being", or the "Great Nest of Being", or even the "Great Chain of Being". The next level is understood, not so much, as rejecting and stepping outside the one previous, as something superior to it and, hence, exercising total control over it (that would constitute a hierarchy in the traditional, derogatory sense), Rather, it reaches beyond it, while embracing it within its compass. As Wilber puts it.

> Reality is a Great Holarchy of Being and Consciousness, reaching from matter to life to mind to spirit. Each dimension transcends and includes its junior dimension in nested holarchy, often represented by concentric circles or spheres.[11]

Wilber is quite convinced that "the perennial philosophy", which enshrines the core of the world's great traditions, would bear him out in this regard. Be that as it may, he recognizes that different cultures may recognize different as members of concentric circles of levels of being, but all are agreed that there are such levels. As for him, he discerns five clear levels, each embracing all that the previous ones contained. Each level or concentric circle represents a qualitatively distinct level of organisation and transcending capacity, while yet integrating and inclusively embracing all its predecessors.[12] The relevant levels are matter/physics, life, mind, soul and spirit.

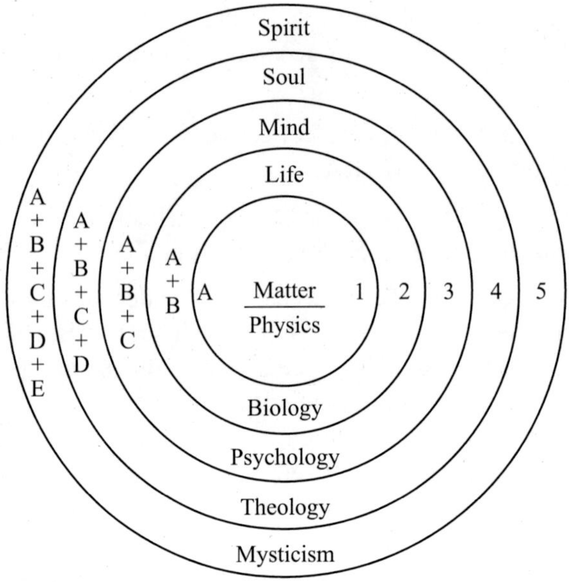

Note: An individual's growth or development, through these levels of consciousness is a fluid affair, not something rigid, liner or discontinuous. Nor is each level a given or something through which we are diver willy-nilly: it's a potential to be freely realized.

Now modernity viewed premodemity (Medieval times, the 'Dark' or 'Middle' Ages) with contempt, as is borne out by the contemptuous terms they used to sum up this complex and otherwise rich moment of European history. Instead of gathering into itself its good points, it threw out everything that belonged to it, in too - the positive and the negative - all to its own loss (Or rather, it tried its level best to remove itself of what it saw as a lot of useless baggage; but, witness Descartes: it's impossible to abdicate ones past – we can't really uproot ourselves from whence we've come). Modernism saw only premodernity's Bad News, as Wilber puts it so colorfully. While rightly rejecting this, it closed its eyes to premodernity's Good News and thereby impoverished itself irreparably.

What exactly was premodernity's Good News? Well, in the first place, it did recognize the Great Chain (Nest) of being in all its radiant glory. It marveled at, and underlined, the depth dimension of Reality (there's more to things than what we can merely sensibly perceive). It saw Reality as multi-layered, not just one-dimensional and monolithic. Furthermore, each of these dimensions is valuable and precious in its own right: the physical, the mental and the spiritual – and each level can be tapped! As for the Bad News, this consisted primarily in the fact that the differentiation and relative autonomy of each quadrant was not noticed: as a result there was domination by the Church of all the other quadrants. Arts, Morals, Science: indeed, everything was fused into one single entity, the Church/Bible. Anyone who questioned the setup was branded and burnt as a heretic. True, the levels of reality were recognized, but not the quadrants and their relative autonomy. Hierarchy in the worst sense of the term, not holarchy, was the name of the game.

Then came postmodernity, a period of enchantment and disenchantment. As a kind of poetic justice, modernism received from the former the same kind of shabby treatment it had doled out to its predecessor. Modernism was represented in purely negative terms. As Wilber summed it up, it' was seen by postmodernism as heralding

> the death of God, the death of the Goddess, the communication of life, the levelling of qualitative distinctions, the brutalities of capitalism, the replacement of quality by quantity, the loss of value and fragmentation of the life world, existential dread, a rampant and vulgar materialism, all of which is aptly summarized in the phrase made famous by Max Weber, the disenchantment of the world.[13]

However, this one-sided assessment of modernism needs a corrective. It did offer some positive points which postmodernism, in its turn, was to ignore at its own peril. What was the enchantment of modernity (once again, to borrow a felicitous phrase from Wilber)? In the first place, it secured the emancipation of the quadrants from the narrow suzerainty of the Church: now Art, Morals and the Sciences discovered the extent of their autonomy and could advance unhindered by monkish interference. Science, now independent, boldly ventured forth and we were blessed with a flood of inventions and discoveries. Arts and Morals move into previously sacrosanct areas and developed ideas and themes that would have once been judged heretical or even sacrilegious, such as liberal democracy, religious freedom and the equality of all people, irrespective of ethnic grouping or religion. Such developments were initially derided and resisted by the Church ... but are now properly enshrined in the documents of Vatican (though there's a mounting groundswell against them instigated by the highest echelons of the ecclesiastical hierarchy). We cannot maintain that the undeniable advances in the positive sciences, together with the abolition of slavery, owed nothing to modernism! This was a Great Enchantment, indeed!

However, modernism ultimately landed us all into a time of Great Disenchantment, too. The autonomy of the quadrants was absolutised. Their inter-dependence became disintegration and each emerged as a law unto itself. Productive differentiation gave way to dissociation, alienation and fragmentation. It was like a game of musical chairs: Science now sat in the throne of domination and began to pronounce tyrannical fatwahs and diktats on Art, Morals, Religion and so on. All quadrants were assimilated to ITS, even humans were reduced to objects: science and pure reason were to be the interpreters and sole criteria of everything. Reality had now become a flatland (another apt Wilberian term), shorn of any depth or multilayerdness.

As Wilber puts it:[14]

> Gone was the mind and gone was spirit – gone, in fact, was the entire Great Chain, except for its pitiful bottom rung – and - in its place, as Whitehead lamented, there was reality as adult affair, soundless, scentless, colorless, merely the hurrying of material, endlessly, endlessly'...

Such a dismal situation has been described variously by different thinkers. Wilber himself termed it "the collapse of the Kosmos", the ultimate disaster of modernism. Habermas saw it as "the colonization of the value spheres by science". Marcuse lamented that "one dimensional man" was born, and Schuon called it "the. desacralisation of the world."[15] If it would be unfair not to congratulate modernism for all its epochal discoveries, it cannot expect to escape universal vituperation for the flatland it created: that was too high a price to pay for its achievements. The postmodernist rebellion was nothing but a (questionable!) attempt to re-enchant the world by once again bringing science, spirituality and art into an integral embrace. This was the positive face of postmodernism: trying to be more inclusive and integrative. It sought to uphold multiculturalism, speaking up for the marginalized and attacking hegemonisation.

Whence emerged interpretation as having a key role to play in human understanding and development. It began to be seen as not only a key to language and literature, but the necessary and only way to go beyond the tip of the iceberg of reality and reach to the very depths of the cosmos itself just as one could study a piece of literature, Hamlet say, on the purely exterior and material level: how much paper and ink were used in writing it, of what chemical substances these were composed and so on? In the same-way, one could: study the cosmos or the human person merely externally and superficially: measure sizes and observe reactions under certain conditions or when exposed to given stimuli – as in modernism. Interpretation – the kind of phenomenological hermeneutics that Paul Ricoeur tries to do – is what postmodernism (at least in intent, if not in deed) tries to do. From all of this, it should be clear how and why interpretation is an indispensable element in the study of the cosmos.

Now, all this is part of the Good News of postmodernism, its "moments of truth", as Wilber would like to put it. These have to be salvaged, for we must not make the same mistakes it did when dealing with modernism: we must not carelessly jettison its good points along with the bad. Let us now take a closer look at the valuable and enduring insights it offers.

There is, first of all, constructivism, that is, it teaches us rightly that "reality is not in all ways pre-given but in some significant ways is a construction, an interpretation."[16] Sometimes what passes for perception, pure and simple, is actually an interpretation. We tend to superimpose 'differences' on integral wholes. Thus we distinguish between the fingers that make up one single hand or divide up the human body into various limbs for convenience. When empiricists call for "strict empirical data" or "only empirical observation" they don't realise that a lot of the rational (mental representation) is inextricably bound up with sensory experience. But, at least in passing, let us draw attention to the hasty generalizations (the exaggerated truths which constitute error) of the postmodernists, we have been careful to hedge what we have called "contextualism" with several cautionary qualifiers, such as "not in all ways", "in some significant-ways" and "sometimes". Postmodernists tended to hurriedly dismiss everything as a mere construct, including both the subject and object (and what 'else is left' after that?)...

This qualified or relative constructivism is sufficient to prick the conceited rubble of those who assume that their particular culture enables them to view reality in an "objective" way, which others, because of their cultures, can't. Hence they take it upon themselves to go aborting such "false" perceptions, by persuasion or by force ("These natives don't even know what's good for them!"), without having to go to the extreme of reducing all things to *mere* constructs!

The next valuable discovery (or re-discovery?) of postmodern is contextualism: contexts do create meaning for us much more than weaned this applies, very specially, once again, to our cultural context ("One man's terrorist is another man's freedom fighter!" is, to some extent true). Saussure is quite right in pointing out that the meaning of a word depends, to a large extent, on its position in a paradigmatic chain. But he is making an unfair generalization when he says that "in language there are only differences, without fixed terms"[17] and concludes (as per his now famous) that the 8.25 express from Geneva" has no fixed meaning in itself: it's a different train that; departs each mom- with different passengers; it can even leave late and it's still called "the 8.25 from Geneva"![18] Hence, the meaning of that phrase does not stem from anything inherent in the term itself, but merely from its position in the time-table: it's after the 7.35 train and before the 9.03 one! Yet, as Christopher Ricks so pointingly asks, can you have pure difference, without differences between things?[19] Is the identity of the express train we are discussing given purely by its position in the railway time-table? As Peter Barry reminds us, the 8.25 from Geneva must be a train and nothing else. No one would say, "There goes the 8.25 Geneva!" were a flock of pigeons to merge reminder the station canopy. Only that which is a train, per se, in itself, would qualify to be called "the 8.25 from Geneva", not every event that manages to squeeze itself between the 7.35 and 9.03 ones!

The final – and momentous – third truth of key importance is what Wilber would hail as "integral aperspectival", borrowing a term from Jean Gebser.[20] This means that no single perspective should be allowed to dominate, or hijack, the multi-dimensional approach to reality (physical, psychological, spiritual, etc). Modernism had – consciously or not – given *carte blanche* to the approach of formal rationality, alone. This is "perspectival rationality", which turned up its nose at all other approaches. Such a privileging perspective generates only a partial, limited and distorted view of reality: only a multi-perspectival approach which privileges none is able to give us a proper vision of the cosmos in all its richness and plurilevel complexity.

Unfortunately, postmodernism blew all these crucial insights and corrections of modernism out of all proportion, an error is an exaggerated truth, whence we get the *Bad News* of postmodernism (the total rejection of foundations, essences and transcendence). Even though this is nothing but the insights carried to erroneous extremes, it would be worth our while to focus on them for a moment.

The first extreme (exaggerated truth) of postmodernism is what we could call interpretationism, i.e., the view that everything is naught but it denies reality to all objective facets of the cosmos. The famous "8.25 from Geneva" is an example of this. Here, postmodernism is but repeating the error of modernism, with a vengeance: it reduces all the quadrants to one!

The second exaggeration results from the total severing of all signifiers from the signified and the referent. It's one thing to say that words (oral sounds assigned to things) are arbitrary? it's even right to castigate modernism for naïvely trying to bind words to reality by means of "rational objective links". But couldn't words be bound to reality of non-rational objective links? Just because rational-objective links can't be established, this doesn't mean that there are no other means to establish objective links with reality! Here, too, post-modernism is not much of an improvement over modernism. If the latter limited reality to it purely external referents (its positivistic measurable dimensions) and denied that it could have any interior aspects,

Postmodernism ended up with what Wilber has aptly called "flatland signifies", reducing reality to language, in the sense of purely external signifies (material marks) with no inner dimensions

Finally, postmodernism merely upholds and glorifies surfaces and recognizes no depth dimension to reality, what Robert Alter said in his review of William H Gass' book, *The Tunnel*,[21] could be applied to postmodernism, at large:[22]

> (E)verything is deliberately reduced to the flattest surface by denying the possibility of making consequential distinct or meaningful ranking of,

moral or aesthetic values. There is no within: murderer or victim, lover and womanist, altruist and bigot, dissolve into the same ineluctable slime.

As I have stated above, postmodernism can't say why we should oppose racism, Nazism or the nor even justify our going to the aid of a woman who's going to be gang-raped or an innocent person about to be lynched by a bullying group of extremists: after all, according to postmodernism, all stances are equal! To sum up, in its haste, postmodernism reduces integral apertspectivism to perspectival madness: the valuable insight that all perspectives are to be given a fair hearing, without any one being privileged is boiled down to the self-contradictory belief that any perspective is as good as the other.

Postmodernism, in other words, had begun with several laudable goals, not the least being to "embrace the Big Three" but it ended up defeating its own purposes and taking a U-turn which landed it back in the same modernistic flatland it had tried to escape. It alighted in a Tower of Babel where cultural relativism and diversity are sought to overcome by a shouting match in which whoever shouts the loudest or uses the biggest stick wins (which is precisely, what it had decried in modernism with its pseudo-justified grand narratives), postmodernism ushers in nihilism, where – under the guise of deconstructionism – all authentic pluralism is effectively reduced to rubble.

What we need is Constructive Postmodernity, which takes the best of Premodernity, Modernity and Postmodernity.

Constructive Postmodernity accepts from Premodernity

- many levels of existence
- divine origin of humans
- the Great Chain of Being

But it rejects

- rigid conservatism
- non-differentiation
- hierarchical oppressionism

Constructive Postmodernity accepts from Modernity

- differentiation of the Big Three
- rapid scientific progress
- cultural progress

it rejects...

- a flatland worldview
- scientific colonialism
- westernism

It takes the best out of Postmodernity

- meaning based on context
- the integral perspective approach
- multiculturism

But it rejects

- exclusive interpretation
- signifier flatland
- depth denial

In summary, constructive postmodernism advocates the AQUAL Matric, i.e., All Quadrants, All Levels, as per this diagram below.

- *Treat all quadrants equally:* give no scope for any to suppress or dominate the others
- *Integrate all Quadrants:* leave them where they are; do not deform themes per one's pet scheme: e.g. force science into morals or religion into science
- *Remember something is true, but only partially so*: for no quadrant or level is the sole or whole truth: EACH CONTAINS BUT A PARTIAL TRUTH!

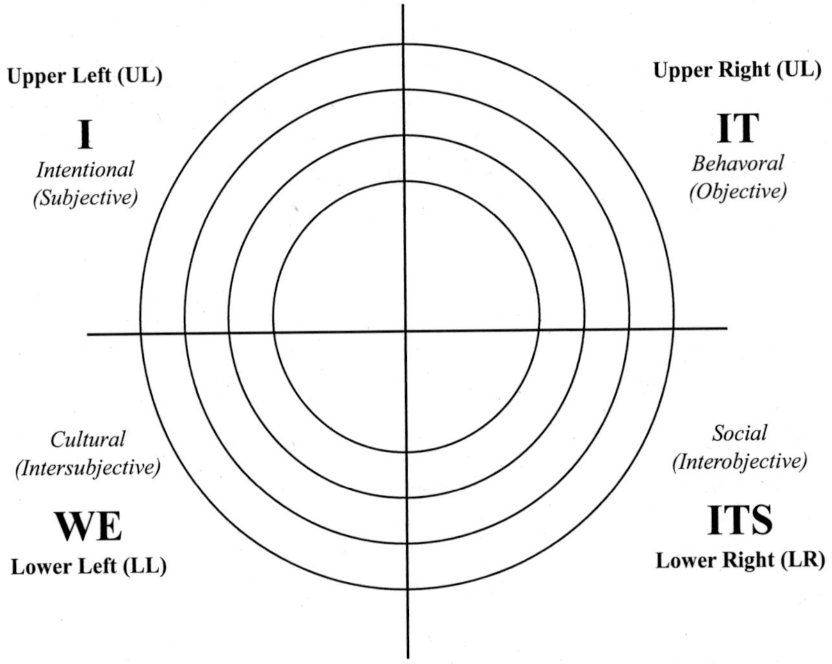

Nor is this attempt to integrate the best of premodernity, modernity and postmodemity a kind of eclecticism. For, as we have observed, Wilber is careful to critique each, reject the inherent defects of each and he has also used them to correct each other. Nor is Wilber contradicting himself as presenting his view as the absolute truth, for he continuously calls' us to critique and modify his approach and seek a yet better paradigm of integration!

Endnotes

1 Aristotle (384-322 BC) introduced the concept of definition. According to Aristotle, the definition of a species consists of *genus proximum* and *differentia specifica*. The *differentia specifica* is that part of the definition not provided by the genus. The genus expresses an "is" or a relationship. Two species with the same genus are said to be members of that genus. The differentia is the attribute by which one species is distinguished from all others of the same genus. Two members of a genus are distinct if and only if their differentiae are distinct. Definition of species within a fixed genus is (not surprisingly) called differentiation.

2 Leibniz, Gottfried Wilhelm, *De Arte Combinatoria* ("On the Art of Combination"), 1666.

3 Lloyd Strickland. *Leibniz's Monadology a New Translation and Guide*. Edinburgh: Edinburgh University Press, 2014.

4 Latin *pace* means "with deference to."

5 Habermas, Jürgen, *The Philosophical Discourse of Modernity* (trans. Frederick Lawrence), Cambridge, The MIT Press, 1996, p. 185 ff.

6 Ibid. See also Rajmohan, George. *Speaking Across Boundaries*, Trivandrum, Carmel International Publishing House, 1998.

7 Habermas, op. cit. p. 294.

8 Wilber, Ken. *The Collected Works of Ken Wilber*. Boston: Shambhala, 1999-2000.

9 Wilber, Ken. *The Spectrum of Consciousness*. Wheaton, IL: Quest Books, 2012 (1976).

10 Wilber has developed this insight in several places. For instance, there is *A Brief History of Everything*, Dublin, Gateway Press, 2001, pp. 64-72. *The Eye of the Spirit*, Boston, Shambhala Press, 1997, pp. 9-13; *Sex, Ecology, Spirituality*, Shambhala Press, 1995, pp. 144149. I am most gratefully indebted to an outstanding student of mine, Agnelo Pinheriro, a brilliant student of mine, who has shown me the relevance of Wilber in any critical study of postmodernism.

11 Wilber, *A Brief History of Everything,* 31-32.

12 The figure can be found in his *The Marriage of Sense and Soul: Integrating Science and Religion*, New York, Random House, p. 8.

13 Cf. Wilber, Ibid. p. 11.

14 Ibid., pp. 56-57.

15 Ibid.

16 That reality is simply given, without an element of construction, is referred to by Weber as "The Myth of the Given". Cf. ibid. p. 121.

17 de Saussure, Ferdinand, *Course in General Linguistics* (trasl. Wade Baskin, London, Fontana/Collins, 1981 (Fourth Impression), p. 120.

18 This, now famous, example is found on page 108 of the above edition.

19 Ricks, Christopher, "In Theory," in *London Review of Books*, April 1981, pp. 3-6; quoted by Peter Barry, *Beginning Theory*, Banchester, The University Press, 1995, p. 45.

20 Wilber also calls this "vision-logic" or "network logic". Cf Jean Gebser, *The Ever-Present Origin* (transl. Noel Basstad and Algis Mickunus, Athens, Ohio University Press, pp. 18- 20.

21 Gass, William H, *The Tunnel,* Alfred A. Knopf, 1995. His magnum opus took 26 years to write and earned him the American Book Award of 1996.

22 Gass' novel is seen as the masterpiece of postmodernism, inasmuch as it is "all surface ... there's no inside however long or far you travel in it, no within, no deep." Cf. Wilber, *The Marriage of Sense and Soul*, pp. 135-136.

APPENDICES

1. THE ACTION OF THE INVADERS

Now the result of this cultural invasion are deep-rooted and destructive – even emasculating, one could say. For it leads to making the invaded feel that they are "culturally inauthentic", that the only way they can become "cultured" is to mimic the cultural values, standards and goals of their invaders: once again, we have the cultural "I" of the invaded (oppressed) person housing the personality of the invader and the duality of the underdog is back with a vengeance.[1]

The Emergence of Authentic Revolutionary Leadership

Invariably, such leaders come from the ranks of former dominators. They are men and women whose existential experience has opened their eyes to the oppressive situation of which they were a part and has led them to seek true solidarity with the oppressed. This would imply sentiments of true commitment and love within them. However, they must make themselves ware of certain "oppressor attitudes" that they still enshrine within their personalities and get rid of them, such as the conviction that they alone know what is best for the people, their tendency to view things from the perspective of the false myths they themselves have propagated, and so on. Thus, the characteristics of dialogical action slowly begin to assert themselves:

a. **Co-operation:** This is marked contrast to the dominating "teacher" making a conquest" of the masses, transforming the vanquished into mere "things". In this approach, the student-teacher and the teacher-students meet in cooperation to transform the world. This does not mean that there is no role for revolutionary leadership in dialogical action; rather, it means that the leaders, however important and crucial their role may be (and is!) derive no right thereby to hustle the people blindly towards their "salvation"! Such a salvation would be a mere gift from the leaders to the people – a breaking of the dialogical bond between them, and in a reduction of the people from being co-authors of liberating action into the objects of that action.[24]

Such co-operation can only be achieved through authentic communication and dialogue and dialogue doesn't manipulate, domesticate or "sloganize". Again, this doesn't mean that the one who dialogues has no goals or objectives; rather is committed to the objective and goal of freedom. Now, it is a contradiction in terms to try and 'conquer the people for freedom: this is but seeking the adhesion of the vanquished to the conqueror's wishes. Just as the antidialogical approach seeks the mythicisation of the world (so as to maintain the status quo), the dialogical approach seeks to unveil it (so as to transform it). Nor can one unveil the world for another: such an action must be done by full-fledged Subjects for themselves!

b. **Organisation**: Just as manipulation was a key element in the antidialogical approach of organisation becomes indispensable for dialogical leaders: this is how they build unity, a unity between the people and their leaders as well as among the people themselves. This calls for "constant, humble and courageous witness" of leaders and people for the common task of liberation. More concretely, this would entail consistency between words and actions, a boldness which doesn't shrink from taking up more or less permanent risks in the struggle for freedom, radicalisation of thought leading to committed action (hence, a far cry from mere 'sectarianism'), faith in the people who are the ultimate Subjects of their own liberation (this implies a sincere and profound love for them and their humanisation). The support of the people may be slow and hesitant in coming, but unless and until it comes there can be no time revolutionary action for justice. Since witness is not an abstract gesture, but an action – a confrontation with the world and with men – it is not static. It is a dynamic element which becomes a part of the societal context in which it occurred; from that moment, it does not cease to affect that context.[2]

Now is the very antithesis of the dominators' 'divide and rule' policy. This is no easy task, also because the dialogical leaders cannot use any of the 'short-cut' methods that the dominators don't scruple to imply, nor have they power on their side. The oppressor aims, at most, to secure some short-term unification of them. So obliging them is to join in the fight against the "common" adversary (the revolutionary leader who is' actually the enemy of only the oppressor)! Since the oppressors are unconcerned about the feelings and opinions of the people, "unity" for them means a mere unity among themselves – something which they can attain quite easily. The revolutionary leader, however, has to seek the more difficult path of communion with the oppressed, combating their inherent "oppressor-oppressed" dualism, integrating their cognitive, affective and active dimensions as full Subjects.

> The objective of dialogical-liberative action is not to 'dislodge' the oppressed from a mythological reality in order to 'bind' them to another reality. On the contrary, the object of dialogical action is to make it possible for the oppressed, by perceiving their adhesion, to opt to transform an unjust reality.[3]

Oppressive or liberative action cannot but have a bearing on "existing" "social structures, which imply certain cultural values. Domination seeks to suffocate and uproot the sociocultural values of the people, as incarnate in their various structures and replace them with those of the oppressors, transplanted into the soil of the oppressed. In liberative action, one seeks to preserve the people's culture inasmuch as these promote and enhance the full flowering of each and every person, irrespective of sex or any other consideration. As and when the people begin to recognize that certain aspects of their structural set-ups do not 'bring this about, they themselves seek to remove them.

Antidialogical cultural action seeks to eradicate the people's culture and replace it with that of the oppressors and, by employing myths (such as that of "God's will"), aims to render permanent and inviolable the transplanted one. They go to the people indirectly (through technology and the mass media), superimposing themselves on the latter, reducing the people to the level of passive spectators, static 'things' who have to be transformed to the advantage of their "betters" Dialogical action involves going to the people directly, building real communion with them and thereby aiming, along with them, to "elicit" liberative action that would humanisingly transform their world.

Those who are invaded, whatever their level, rarely go beyond the models which the invaders prescribe for them. In cultural synthesis, there are no invaders; hence, there are no imposed models. In their stead, there are actors who critically analyze reality (never separating this analysis from action) and intervene as Subjects in the historical process.[4]

Only in cultural synthesis is the opposition between the world-view of the people and that of their leaders resolved – to the enrichment of both. And the only way to this is by meeting, dialogue and mutual challenge. In the antidialogical theory of action, cultural invasion serves the end of manipulation, which in turn serves the ends of con – quest, and conquest serves the ends of domination. Cultural synthesis serves the ends of organization; organisation serves the ends of liberation.

Conclusion

Now that the wheel has gone full circle, illumined by Freire's telling analysis of revolution, we can cry out, in mock paraphrase of Madame Roland as she mounted the steps to the guillotine during those heady days of the French Revolution and which can be found on the opening pages of this text, “O, Revolutionaries and Liberators, what crimes are committed in your name?” Freire’s compelling words throw light on why so many terrorist organizations, from the ETA to the Taliban, end up only adding more suffering and oppression to the people they claim to liberate and sometimes, with the best of intentions, do but substitute one group of feeling less and merciless dominators with another, while the condition of the .oppressed remains the same ... if not gets progressively worse.

Endnotes

1 Freire, Paulo, *Pedagogy of the Oppressed*, New York : Continuum, 2000, pp. 121-122.

2 Ibid. p. 144.

3 Ibid. p. 141.

4 Ibid. p. 148.

2. CYRIL DESBRUSLAIS, SJ: A PHILOSOPHER OF LIBERATION

Life of an effective counsellor, committed teacher and an accomplished playwright

- Born in Calcutta on 21 December 1940.
- He was schooled at Calcutta and Asanol
- He did his Bachelor of Commerce at St Xavier's College
- Worked for a year at Remington Rand of India.
- He was inspired to join the Society of Jesus through his Uncle, Fr Vernon Desbruslais SJ, in 1962.
- Philosophy Studies 1965-1968 (DNC-JDV, then called the Papal Athenaeum)
- 1968-70 MA (English Lit) Pune University
- Theology Studies 1971-1975 (DNC - JDV)
- Doctoral Studies Sorbonne, France
- Taught for some years at JDV then defended his thesis in 1983
- 35 years of teaching Philosophy in Various Seminaries and Institutions
- He has taught all the major philosophy courses except epistemology, logic and cosmology.
- Like existential philosophers, he has been presenting his philosophy in over 48 plays, written and directed by him.
- Presently, residing at St Vincent College, Pune as *Professor emeritus.*

Inspired by:

Basic inspiration - St Ignatius of Loyola
Pedro Arrupe SJ
Adolfo Nicolás SJ
Pierre Teilhard de Chardin SJ (who was his professor)

Inspired:

Countless young people, including Shashi Tharoor, former Minister of External Affairs, and General Shankar Roychowdhury, former Chief of the Army Staff.

Mentor of Searching and Serving in Unity:

- Started in 1971, when he was beginning his Theology studies at De Nobili College, Pune, India.
- **Reason:** His own youth had been very much of a mess and he didn't want other youngsters to have to go through what he did, making the same foolish mistakes, which invariably rendered one all the more hurt, confused and lonely.

- **Aim:** To reach out to those youngsters who came from broken families, bunked class, and had "bad habits" – in short, never joined any youth groups of their own volition.

To welcome non-Christians and those of no particular religious persuasion and to celebrate our differences, not just sweep them under the carpet by having inter-faith celebrations of our major feasts.

Qualities Needed for a Youth Animator

- One needs a soft heart, to be able to *feel with* youngsters the hurt, awkwardness and confusion they are going through and at the same time, a tough skin, so as not be too easily discouraged when things don't seem to go too well.
- Don't wait for them to come near you when they have problems but be ready to go out to them, where they are and spend time with them, apparently "waste time" with them. Let them know that you love them.

Philosophy of Life

- Life is for being more human than for having more things, having more money, having more power, etc.
- We should develop the "be-attitudes", an attitude of being as Jesus lived "though he was in the form of God, did not count equality with God a thing to be grasped, but emptied himself, by taking the form of a servant, being born in the likeness of men. And being found in human form, he humbled himself by becoming obedient to the point of death, even death on a cross." (Phil 2: 48)

Philosophy of Liberation

India needs a Philosophy of Liberation than a theology of Liberation because we need united action for justice and liberation by ALL Indians, inspired with a common vision. And this common vision could NOT be the Holy Book of one religion, but a shared understanding of the human person. This is not oppressive understanding of anything but a liberative understanding which helps us to be "fully human, fully alive."

About Present Formation System

Those students who have showed to be mature should be given the mission to live outside the campus or religious houses with poor, ordinary people. This will help them to "be more human."

On Broken trust between individuals and religious groups

Let's give people context for meaningful relationships. Don't try to dominate in any relation. Be open to differences and celebrate the differences in other's traditions.

On Contemporary Social Issues

What is happening in India today is overstress on Uniformity. Unity without diversity is uniformity, and that's boring; diversity without beauty is jarring and garish, and that's ugly. It had happened in Catholic Church also. Each of us have to learn how to better and appreciate our faith and culture more by being more open to, and learning from, the views of others.

Message to Budding Philosophers

Philosopher should not over-intellectualize or rationalize. They should be down to earth and live their life deeply and celebrate it in the liturgy so that people may learn and understand it in a better way.

Interview conducted by OIC, OSJ and SSS Brothers of III BPh (2015-2017 Batch), headed by Alexis P broalexisoic@gmail.com. Clearer graphics is available with the author Br Alexis or with editor (kuru@jdv.edu.in).

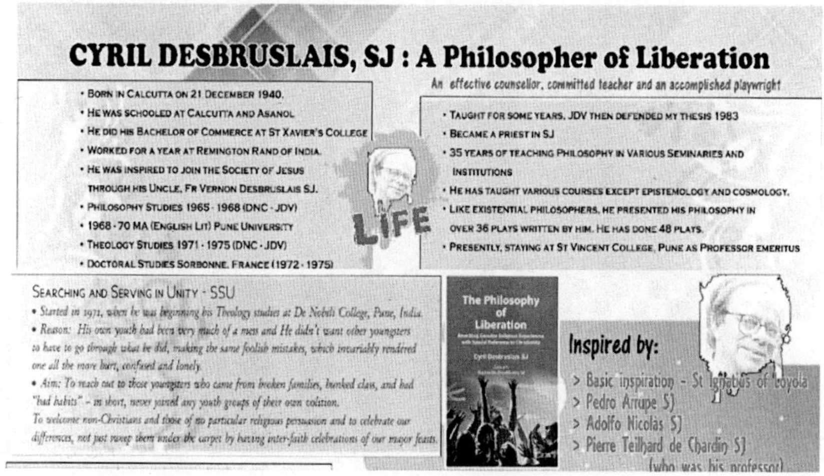

Qualities needed for a youth Animator
• One needs a soft heart, to be able to feel with youngsters the hurt, awkwardness and confusion they are going through and at the same time, a tough skin, so as not be too easily discouraged when things don't seem to go too well.
• Don't wait for them to come near you when they have problems but be ready to go out to them, where they are and spend time with them, apparently "waste time" with them. Let them know that you love them.
About Present Formation System ...
Those students who have showed to be mature should be given the mission to live outside the campus or religious houses with poor, ordinary people.
This will help them to "be more human."
CYRIL DESBRUSLAIS
Philosophy of life
• Life is for being more human than for having more- having more things, having more money, having more power, etc.
• We should develop "be-attitude", an attitude of being as Jesus lived "though he was in the form of God, did not count equality with God a thing to be grasped, but emptied himself, by taking the form of a servant, being born in the likeness of men. And being found in human form, he humbled himself by becoming obedient to the point of death, even death on a cross." (Phil 2: 4-8)
Philosophy of Liberation
Broken trust between individuals and religious groups
Give people context for meaningful relationships.
Don't try to dominate in any relation.
Be open to differences and celebrate the differences.
India needs a Philosophy of Liberation than a theology of Liberation because we need united action for justice and liberation by ALL Indians, inspired with a common vision. And this common vision could NOT be the Holy Book of one religion, but a shared understanding of the human person. This is not oppressive understanding of anything but a liberative understanding which helps us to be " fully human, fully alive."
On Contemporary Social Issues ...
What is happening in India today is over stress on Uniformity. Unity without diversity is uniformity, and that's boring; diversity without beauty is jarring and garish, and that's ugly. It had happened in Catholic Church also. Each of us Have to learn how to better and appreciate our faith and culture more by being more open to, and learning from, the views of others.
Message to budding Philosophers ...
A Philosopher should not over intellectualize or rationalize. They should be down to earth and live their life deeply and celebrate it in the liturgy so that people may learn and understand it in a better way.
Prepared By: OIC, OSJ and SSS Brothers of III B. Ph

GLOSSARY

Acosmism: Acosmism, in contrast to pantheism, denies the reality of the universe, seeing it as ultimately illusory, (the prefix "a-" in Greek meaning negation; like "un-" in English), and only the infinite unmanifest Absolute is real. Conceptual versions of Acosmism are found both in Eastern and Western philosophies.

Against the grain: different from what is normal or usual. It takes courage to go against the grain and stand up for what you believe in.

Archē is that primeval stuff out of which all things were made. The pre-Socratic philosophy was in search of this stuff that led to the origin of everything.

Arche-writing: The term 'arche-writing' is used by Derrida to describe a form of language which cannot be conceptualized within the 'metaphysics of presence.' Arche-writing is an original form of language which is not derived from speech.

Beverley Hills: A city of southern California surrounded by Los Angeles. It adjoins Hollywood and is famous as a fashionable residential area for show business personalities.

Chora: (χώρα) was the territory of the Ancient Greek polis outside the city proper. The term has been used in philosophy by Plato to designate a receptacle (as a "third kind" [triton genos]; Timaeus 48e4), a space, a material substratum, or an interval. The earliest stage in your psychosexual development (0-6 months), according to Julia Kristeva. In this pre-lingual stage of development, you were dominated by a chaotic mix of perceptions, feelings, and needs. You did not distinguish your own self from that of your mother or even the world around you. Rather, you spent your time taking into yourself everything that you experienced as pleasurable without any acknowledgment of boundaries. This is the stage, then, when you were closest to the pure materiality of existence, or what Lacan terms "the Real." At this stage, you were, according to Kristeva, purely dominated by your drives (both life drives and the death drives)

Circumfession: The nearest Derrida came to giving us his personal credo is in his Circumfession, in 1993 (the coined word is, in itself, provocative enough): here he evokes his, "religion, about which nobody understands anything, any more than my mother, who asked other people a while ago, not daring to speak to me about it, if I believed in God. ... but she must have known that the constancy of God in my life is called by other names, so that I quite rightly pass for an atheist, the omnipresence to me of what I call God in my absolved private language being that neither of an eye-witness nor that of a voice doing anything than talking to me with-out saying anything."

Contextualism: it is the doctrine which emphasizes the importance of the context of enquiry in a particular question. Contexts do create meaning for us much more than weaned this applies, very specially, once again, to our cultural context.

Dadaism: A European artistic and literary movement (1916-1923) that flouted conventional aesthetic and cultural values by producing works marked by nonsense, travesty, and incongruity. [French dada, hobbyhorse, Dada, of baby-talk origin.] This *avant-garde* art movement started in the early 20th century, with early centers in Zürich, Switzerland.

Deconstruction: Originated by the philosopher Jacques Derrida, deconstruction is an approach to understanding the relationship between text and meaning. Derrida's approach consisted of conducting readings of texts with an ear to what runs counter to the intended meaning or structural unity of a particular text.

Différance: "difference and deferral of meaning." According to Derrida it is the impossibility of any sign within a system of signs having a fixed meaning; the process by which meaning is endlessly deferred from one sign to another within such a system.

Disenchantment with the world: In social science, disenchantment (German: *Entzauberung*) is the cultural rationalization and devaluation of mysticism apparent in modern society. Max Weber uses the concept of disenchantment to describe the character of modernized, bureaucratic, secularized Western society, where scientific understanding is more highly valued than belief, and where processes are oriented toward rational goals, as opposed to traditional society where for Weber "the world remains a great enchanted garden."

Doubling the text: Doubling of commentary is the interpretation (by the reader) of the writer's conscious or intentional meaning. Derrida scornfully refers to the illusory and useless interpretation or "reproduction of the text" as "doubling the text"

Enlightenment: European intellectual movement of the late 17th and 18th centuries emphasizing reason and individualism rather than tradition. It was heavily influenced by 17th-century philosophers such as Descartes, Locke, and Newton, and its prominent figures included Kant, Goethe, Voltaire, Rousseau, and Adam Smith. The Enlightenment presented a challenge to traditional religious views. Enlightenment thinkers were the liberals of their day.

Évenemants (events) of 1789: The French Revolution from 1789 to 1799 led to the end of the monarchy, and to many wars. King Louis XVI was executed in 1793. The revolution ended when Napoleon Bonaparte took power in November 1799.

Évenements (events) of 1968: The volatile period of civil and political unrest in France during May 1968 was punctuated by demonstrations and major general strikes as well as the occupation of universities and factories across France. At its height, it brought the economy of France almost to a halt. It was mostly led by the students and most of the postmodern thinkers were directly involved in it. Also called student rebellion.

Female, Feminine, feminist: It is to Toril Moi and her insights on 'conditioning' and 'socialisation' that we are indebted for the now well-worn triple distinction between feminist, female and feminine: she defines these, respectively as, 'a political position' (the demand for women's share in the power usurped totally by men) 'a matter of biology' (the physiological fact of having certain sexual organs) and 'a set of culturally defined characteristics' (a construct, varying from culture to culture, but invariably determined by the dominant male ethos). Simone de Beauvoir is obviously using 'woman' in the last-named sense when she stages in the opening lines of her *The Second Sex*, "One is not born a woman, one becomes a woman."

Gaze: The postcolonial gaze "has the function of establishing the subject/object relationship ... ... Utilizing postcolonial gaze theory allows formerly colonized societies to overcome the socially constructed barriers that often prohibit them from expressing their true cultural, social, economic, and political rights.

Gender and sex: See Sex and gender.

Genre: A style or category of art, music, or literature. It is characterized by similarities in form, style, or subjet matter. The four main literary genres are poetry, fiction, nonfiction, and drama, with each varying in style, structure, subject matter and the use of figurative language.

Grand narratives: A narrative is a story that functions to legitimize power, authority, and social customs. A grand narrative or metanarrative is one that claims to explain various events in history, gives meaning by connecting disperse events and phenomena by appealing to some kind of universal knowledge or schema. The term grand narratives (*grands récits*) can be applied to a wide range of thoughts which includes Marxism, religious doctrines, belief in progress, universal reason, and others. Its opposite the mini or little narratives (*petitsrécites*) try to explain the world to a smaller and limited community.

Hauntology: A portmanteau of haunting and ontology, it refers to a state of temporal, historical, and ontological disjunction in which presence is replaced by a deferred non-origin, represented by "the figure of the ghost as that which is neither present, nor absent, neither dead nor alive."

Holarchy: A holarchy is a connection between holons, where a holon is both a part and a whole. The term was coined in Arthur Koestler's 1967 book The Ghost in the Machine. Holarchy is commonly referred to as a form of hierarchy; however, hierarchy, by its definition, has both an absolute top and bottom.

Integral aperspectival: This means that no single perspective should be allowed to dominate, or hijack, the multi-dimensional approach to reality (physical, psychological, spiritual, etc). Modernism had – consciously or not – given carte blanche to the approach of formal rationality, alone. This is "perspectival rationality", which turned up its nose at all other approaches. Such a privileging perspective generates only a partial, limited and distorted view of reality: only a multi-perspectival approach which privileges none is able to give us a proper vision of the cosmos in all its richness and plurilevel complexity.

Little narratives: Or *petits récites*, See Metanarrative (*Grands récits* or big stories).

Logcentrism: According to Derrida, "logocentrism" is the attitude that logos (the Greek term for speech, thought, law, or reason) is the central principle of language and philosophy.

Logocentrism is the view that speech, and not writing, is central to language.

Metanarrative: A metanarrative (also meta-narrative and grand narrative; French: méta récit or grand récit) in postmodernism is a narrative about narratives of historical meaning, experience, or knowledge, which offers a society legitimation through the anticipated completion of a (as yet unrealized) master idea. This term developed by Jean-François Lyotard to mean a theory that tries to give a totalizing, comprehensive account to various historical events, experiences, and social, cultural phenomena based upon the appeal to universal truth or universal values.

Middle ages: The period of European history from the fall of the Roman Empire in the West (5th century) to the fall of Constantinople (1453), or, more narrowly, from *c.* 1000 to 1453. It is also called the Dark Ages.

Modern philosophy: Modern philosophy is philosophy developed in the modern era and associated with modernity. It is not a specific doctrine or school (and thus should not be confused with Modernism), although there are certain assumptions common to much of it, which helps to distinguish it from earlier philosophy. René Descartes is generally considered the father of modern philosophy. He was the first major figure in the philosophical movement known as rationalism, a method of understanding the world based on the use of reason as the means to attain knowledge.

Modernism is a philosophical movement that, along with cultural trends and changes, arose from wide-scale and far-reaching transformations in Western society during the late 19th and early 20th centuries.

Monoformism: Raimundo Panikkar referred to this type of colonial thinking as an attempt at a gross "monoformism" of culture (i.e. the resolve to give one single Western/"Christian" shape to the rich plurality of world cultures).

Nihilism: It is the belief that life has no intrinsic meaning or value. With respect to the universe, existential nihilism posits that a single human or even the entire human species is insignificant, without purpose and unlikely to change in the totality of existence.

Onomatopoeia: It is the process of creating a word that phonetically imitates, resembles, or suggests the sound that it describes. As such words are uncountable nouns, onomatopoeia refers to the property of such words.

Paradigmatic axis: The distinction is a key one in structuralist semiotic analysis. These two dimensions are often presented as 'axes', where the horizontal axis is the syntagmatic and the vertical axis is the paradigmatic.

Paralogy: a method or process of reasoning which contradicts logical rules or formulas, especially the use of a faulty syllogism (the formal fallacy).

Referent: the thing in the world (reality) that a word or phrase denotes or stands for.

Renaissance: the revival of European art and literature under the influence of classical models in the 14th–16th centuries. It started as a cultural movement in Italy in the Late Medieval period and later spread to the rest of Europe. The Renaissance was important because it ushered in many changes, particularly in European art and culture. The Renaissance is generally understood to be the art, literature and culture accumulated in the 14th to 16th centuries. *Sapere Aude: Sapereaude* is the Latin phrase meaning "Dare to know"; and also is loosely translated as "Dare to be wise", or even more loosely as "Dare to think for yourself!" ... The phrase is widely used as a motto, especially by educational institutions.

Semiotic language: Semiotic language, according to Kristeva, is more feminine, redolent with 'displacement, slippage, condensation'. It is less logical (if at all!) and prefers random connections and polysemy. It is the language of poetry and of conversation. Symbolic language is that of scientific research and exactitude, 'plain, unadorned writings', as the eighteenth century rationalists would say. It is opened to symbolic language. The semiotic is in excess of the "symbolic"

Sex and gender: The distinction between sex and gender is between a person's biological sex (the anatomy of an individual's reproductive system, and secondary sex characteristics) from that person's gender, which can refer to either social roles based on the sex of the person (gender role) or personal identification of one's own.

Signified: The terms signified and signifier are most commonly related to semiotics, which is defined by Oxford Dictionaries Online as "the study of signs and symbols and their use or interpretation". Ferdinand de Saussure was one of the two founders of semiotics. His book, *Course in General Linguistics* is considered to be one of the most influential books published in the twentieth century". Saussure explained that a sign was not only a sound-image but also a concept. Thus he divided the sign into two components: the signifier (or "sound-image") and the signified (or "concept").. For Saussure, the signified and signifier were purely psychological; they were form rather than substance. Today the signifier is interpreted as the material form (something which can be seen, heard, touched, smelled or tasted) and the signified as the mental concept. For postmodernism the signified refers to not to a reality outside.

Signifier: See Signified

Situationism: It is an artistic and political movement started emerging during the early 1960s in France. This movement experimented with the idea of constructing a situation – hence the name. Constructing a situation was setting up an environment favorable for the fulfillment of a particular desire.

Simulacrum: an image or representation of someone or something. a slight, unreal, or vague semblance of something; superficial likeness, according to Baudrillard.

Simulations: the production of a computer model of something, especially for the purpose of study. In postmodernism this theme was introduced by Baudrillard.

Sous rapture: Derrida' uses "*sous rapture*" which translates from the French to "under erasure" defines this process more thoroughly. "This is to write a word, cross it out, and then print both word and deletion. (Since the word is inaccurate, it is crossed out. Since it is necessary, it remains legible)". In other words, we must twist and contort available resources (such as language) in order to do reach a different perspective. "We must learn to use and erase our language at the same time." Some concepts are difficult to accurately describe since they are 'non-concepts rather than 'concepts', because, once we 'conceptify' them, we forthwith invest them with attributes like stability and permanence and objectivity, all of which would fly in the face of what they would represent. So either we call them 'concepts' *sous rature*. or 'concepts or 'non-concepts'.

Supplément : In French *supplément* means what it means in English: something which adds to, or completes, what was in another thing (an interpretation "*suppléments*" a text in the sense that it makes its meaning more clear). But it has also another sense in French, that of a replacement, in the sense that language re-places or stands in for reality. So Derrida asks: In what sense can language "stand in" for reality, given that language is something we inherit, with its own history, philosophy and rules (langue) already "built in", as it were?

Svelteness: Lyotard coined this term to describe the way the individual can best challenge entrenched systems of cultural and social repression. It is "guerrilla-like attitude of flexible and creative response to pressures emanating from one's particular grand narrative – the ability to 'go to a ball in the evening and fight a war at dawn,' as Lyotard rather romantically puts it."

Syntagmatic analysis (chain or axes): In semiotics, syntagmatic analysis is analysis of syntax or surface structure (syntagmatic structure) as opposed to paradigms (paradigmatic analysis). ... Of particular use in semiotic study, a syntagm is a chain which leads, through syntagmatic analysis, to an understanding of how a sequence of events forms a narrative. A paradigmatic relation is a relation that holds between elements of the same category, i.e., elements that can be substituted for each other. It contrasts with syntagmatic relation, which applies to relations holding between elements that are combined with each other.

Weltanschauung: The *German* word Weltanschauung literally means "world view"; it combines "Welt" ("world") with "*Anschauung*" ("view"), which ultimately derives from the Middle High German verb *schouwen* ("to look at" or "to see"). This may be contrasted to *Weltbild*, which is the picture of the world.

BIBLIOGRAPHY

Barry, Peter, *Beginning Theory*, Banchester, The University Press, 1995.

Barthes, Roland, Riva Miller, and Ron Howard. *The Pleasure of the Text.* Oxford: Blackwell, 1990.

Baudrillard, Jean, *America*. Milano: SE, 2009.

Baudrillard, Jean, *Cool Memories*. 1990.

Brooker, Peter (ed.), *Modernism/Postmodernism*. London, Longman, 1992.

Ciapolo, Roman T. (ed), *Postmodernism and Christian Philosophy*. New York, Random House, 1991.

da Silva, Antony, "Combatting Communalism in Twenty-First Century India: A Social-Psychological Perspective", *Jnanadeepa: Pune Journal of Religious Studies*. Vol. 2, No. 1 (January 1999).

de Onis y Sanchez, Federico, Antologfa de la poesfaespaflola e hispano-americanna (1881 - 1932). 1934. Illathuparampil, p. 612, footnote 25.

de Saussure, Ferdinand, *Course in General Linguistics* (trasl. Wade Baskin, London, Fontana/Collins, 1981 (Fourth Impression).

Derrida, Jacques, *Of Grammatology* (trsl. Gayatri Chakravorty Spivak), Delhi, Motilal Banarsidass Publishers, 1994.

Desbruslais, Cyril, *The Philosophy of Religion.* Pune, Jnana-Deepa Vidyapeeth, 2008.

Desbruslais, Cyril, *Modern Philosophy*. Mimeographed Text (no date), Pune, Jnana-Deepa Vidyapeeth.

Descartes, Rene, *Discourse on Method. Part I.*

Fillingham, Lydia Alix, *Foucault for Beginners*. Hyderabad. Orient Longman, 2000, p. 67.

Freire, Paulo, *Pedagogy of the Oppressed.* New York: Continuum, 2000.

Gass, William H., *The Tunnel,* Alfred A. Knopf, 1995. His magnum opus took 26 years to write and earned him the American Book Award of 1996.

Gebser, Jean, *The Ever-Present Origin* (transl. Noel Basstad and Algis Mickunus) Athens, Ohio University Press.

Gregorios, Paulos Mar, "Modern, Postmodern, and the Future of the Humanity: Nostalgia for the Unattainable." http://www.paulosmargregorios.in/Work_of_Mar_Gregorios/English%20Articles/Humanity/ modern_postmodern.htm

Habermas, Jürgen, *The Philosophical Discourse of Modernity* (trans. Frederick Lawrence), Cambridge, The MIT Press, 1996.

Hart, Kevin, "Jacques Derrida; The God Effect", in *Post-Secular Philosophy* (Phillip Blond, ed.), Routledge, London and New York, 1998, p. 261.

Huxley, Aldous. *Brave New World.* New York: Spark Publishing, 2014.

Johnson, Barbara, *The Critical Difference*. Johns Hopkins University Press, 1980, p. 5.

Johnson, Barbara, *The Critical Difference*. Johns Hopkins University Press, 1980. p. 25.

Kellner, Douglas and Jean Baudrillard; *From Marxism to Postmodernism and Beyond.* Cambridge and Oxford, Polity and Blackwell, 1989.

Kolb, David, *The Critique of Pure Modernity: Hegel, Heidegger and After*. Chicago, The University of Chicago Press, 1986.

Lakeland, Paul, *Postmodemity: A Christian Identity in a Fragmented World.* Minneapolis, Fortress Press, 1997.

Lechte, John, *Julia Kristeva*. London, Routledge, 1990.

Leibniz, Gottfried Wilhelm, and Lloyd Strickland, *Leibniz's Monadology: A New Translation and Guide*. Edinburgh: Edinburgh University Press, 2014.

Leibniz, Gottfried Wilhelm, *De Arte Combinatoria* ("On the Art of Combination"), 1666.

Lévi-Strauss, Claude, *La Geste D'Asdiwal*. Paris, Imprimerie Nationale, 1958.

Lévi-Strauss, Claude. *The View from Afar*. Chicago: University of Chicago Press, 1992.

Lyotard, Jean-François, *The Postmodern Condition: A Report on Knowledge*. Minneapolis, Minn: Univ. of Minnesota Press, 2010.

Marks & de Courtivron, *New French Feminism*. New York, Harvester, 1981.

Pandikattu, Kuruvilla. *Postmodernity: An Indian Appraisal*. New Delhi: Serials Publ, 2008.

Pannwitz, Rudolf, *Die Krisis der europaischen Kultur*. 1917 as cited by Mathew Illathuparampil in *Vidyajyoti*. Vol. 5, No. 8 (August 2001).

Powell, Jim, *Derrida for Beginners*. Hyderabad, Orient Longman, 2000.

Puthenpurackal, Johnson J., "Postmodernity and its Effects of Metaphysics", a paper presented to the Association of Christian Philosophers of India (October 27 - 29 October, 1999).

Pylee, M. V., "Religion and the Modernist Movement," in Thomas Paul (ed) *Present Day Challenges to Religion*, Alwaye, Pontifical Institute of Theology and Philosophy, 1973,p. 32.

Rajmohan, George, *Speaking across Boundaries*, Trivandrum, Carmel International Publishing House, 1998.

Ricks, Christopher, "In Theory," in *London Review of Books*, April 1981, pp. 3-6.

Sarup, Madan, *An Introductory Guide to Post-Structuralism and Postmodernism.* Athens, Georgia, The University of Georgia Press, 1993.

Sim, Stuart (ed.), *The A-Z Guide to Modem Literary and Cultural Theorists.* London, Prentice Hall, 1995, p. 271.

Sim, Stuart (ed.), *The A-Z Guide to Modern Literary and Cultural Theories.* London, Prentice Hall, 1951.

Taylor, Victor E. and Charles E. Winquist (editors), *Encyclopedia of Postmodernism.* London, Routledge, 2001, "Introduction", p. xiii.

van Niekirk, Anton A., "Post-Metaphysical versus Postmodern Thinking", in *Philosophy Today* (Summer 1995).

Wilber, Ken, *The Marriage of Sense and Soul: Integrating Science and Religion.* New York, Random House.

Wilber, Ken, *A Brief History of Everything.* Dublin, Gateway Press, 2001.

Wilber, Ken, *Sex, Ecology, Spirituality.* Shambhala Press, 1995.

Wilber, Ken, *The Eye of the Spirit.* Boston, Shambhala Press, 1997.

Wilber, Ken, *The Spectrum of Consciousness.* Wheaton, IL: Quest Books, 2012 (1976).

Wilber, Ken. *The Collected Works of Ken Wilber.* Boston: Shambhala, 1999-2000.

Wollstonecraft, Mary. *A Vindication of the Rights of Woman.* Aberdeen: Ockham Publishing, 2015.